Healing in
the Spirit

Jim McManus

D1407432

a redemptorist publication

Published by **Redemptorist Publications**

Copyright © 2002 Redemptorist Publications

Cover design: Orchid Design
Design: Rosemarie Pink

New Revised Edition November 2002

ISBN 0 85231 265 2

Printed by Estudios Gráficos Zure, Spain

Redemptorist
P U B L I C A T I O N S

Alphonsus House Chawton Hampshire GU34 3HQ
Telephone 01420 88222   Fax 01420 88805
rp@ShineOnline.net   www.ShineOnline.net

Contents

Introduction to the New Edition

A team of scientists at Aberdeen University received funding from the Scottish Executive on 12 November 2001 to investigate the claims of "spiritual healing". Dr Arrun Sharma, the director of the project, said, "Spiritual healing is now one of the many complementary therapies that are now getting to the stage where they have to demonstrate their effectiveness and undergo the same scientific process that any treatment does in the health service." This is a major development in a British university and the new Scottish Parliament in Edinburgh. It is recognition that those who undertake the medical care of the community should no longer ignore the spiritual dimension.

Medical researchers in America have been amassing evidence over the past twenty years on the healing power of intercessory prayer. Herbert Benson, a professor of medicine at Harvard University, recently published a book entitled *Timeless Healing* in which he develops the thesis that the human being is "hard wired for God" and that intercessory prayer has a healing effect in sickness. For the past thirty years Dr Benson has been working at the interface of medicine and spirituality, of medical treatment and intercessory prayer. And he can write, with refreshing simplicity and humility, "My patients have taught me a great deal about the opportunities that emerge when artificial barriers are broken down, and how physical ailments inspire soul-searching and a revival of meaningful living, and about how the human spirit enlivens and transforms the body."[1]

The healing ministry, which had, up until recently, very little support either in the medical world or sadly in the Church, now has strong supporters in many medical schools and teaching hospitals. Dr Larry Dossey tells us that "Courses on the role of religious devotion and prayer in healing are currently being taught in approximately fifty

U.S. medical schools. This is a historic event, a stunning reversal of the exclusion of these factors from medical education for the most of the twentieth century."[2] Wouldn't it be a supreme irony if doctors in the future felt more comfortable than priests and lay ministers in praying for healing? How many priests would feel at ease preaching what Dr Harold Koenig of Duke University Medical Center teaches, Namely: "Lack of religious involvement has an effect on mortality that is equivalent to forty years of smoking one pack of cigarettes per day."[3]

Two scientists, Andrew Newberg and Eugene D'Aquili, write:

> Until 1994, for example, the American Psychiatric Association officially classified "strong religious belief" as a mental disorder. New data, however, indicates that religious beliefs and practices can improve mental and emotional health in several significant ways. For example, research shows that rates of drug abuse, alcoholism, divorce, and suicide are much lower among religious individuals than among the population at large. It also seems clear that people who practice religion are much less likely to suffer from depression and anxiety than the population at large, and that they recover more quickly when they do. Other experiments have linked specific religious activities to positive psychological results; spiritual practices such as meditation, prayer, or participation in devotional services, have been shown to reduce feelings of anxiety and depression significantly, boost self-esteem, improve the quality of interpersonal relationships, and generate a more positive outlook on life.[4]

The scientific and medical world, so long closed to the spiritual, is now open to and ready for partnership with spiritual practitioners. Dr Elizabeth McSherry, a former professor of clinical paediatrics at the University of California, San Francisco, has researched the effect of pastoral care on patients in hospitals. She discovered that

> Major open-heart surgery patients who received the special daily chaplain visits averaged an impressive two-day decrease in length of stay, compared with their counterparts who did not receive the specialized pastoral intervention. And the patients receiving the extra pastoral care also suffered less postsurgery depression, a finding which has great potential significance, given what we have discovered about the relationship between depression and coronary artery disease.[5]

The scientific world of medicine is now beginning to take the spiritual world of faith seriously. Science does not seek to determine what faith is. It accepts faith as a given. After releasing the findings of extensive research into the relationship between faith and a healthy immune system, Harold Koenig said to reporters: "We're not trying to prove that there is a higher power. But maybe believing in that higher power could be an important key to people's health."[6] What scientists are beginning to study is the power of the very act of believing in itself. Making an act of faith in God, or in God as you conceive God, or in a "higher power" is now seen as beneficial for the whole immune system. Faith and science can now enter into a constructive dialogue in caring for the whole person. For too long the domain of faith was restricted to the dimension of the soul while the body was seen as the exclusive preserve of science. While faith got on with "saving the soul" science got on with the business of "saving the body". That old "division of labour", based as it was on the false dichotomy between body and soul, is no longer tenable. Modern medicine today seeks to care for the whole person while spirituality today is holistic in its approach, that is, it too seeks the welfare of the whole person. Wilkie Au gives us a very good description of holistic spirituality:

> A holistic spirituality is a religious outlook as well as a way of structuring one's life in order to embody religious values. As a religious orientation, it asks the question, "How is God leading and loving us in all aspects of our lives?" It is holistic insofar as it acknowledges that all aspects of a person's life must be subjected to the transforming influence of the Spirit. In the past, certain spiritualities restricted the scope of the spiritual life to one's relationship to God and the condition of one's soul. In contrast, a holistic spirituality attempts to embrace the totality of a person's existence, including one's relationship with others, with one's work, and with the material world. Defining the spiritual life as coextensive with life itself, it finds every human concern relevant. God's spirit dwells and acts in every aspect of our lives and not merely in such explicitly religious activities as prayer and worship. [7]

As both medicine and spirituality take a more holistic approach to their subject, to the person, they find common ground for the healing and the wholeness of life. Medicine, by opening itself to the spiritual dimension of the person, is rediscovering the healing power of prayer and faith, while spirituality, by taking the physical body and its concomitants more seriously, is rediscovering the whole incarnational dimension of faith. We can only address "the soul" by taking the body seriously. The relationship between our material reality, our body, and our spiritual reality, our soul and spirit, has been the subject of intense philosophical and theological debate throughout history. The official teaching of the Church today is well expressed in the new Catechism:

> The unity of soul and body is so profound that one has to consider the soul to be the "form" of the body: i.e., it is because of its spiritual soul that the body made of matter becomes a living body; spirit and matter, in man, are not two natures united, but rather their union forms a single nature. [8]

The human person is a unity of "body and soul". We cannot split this unity and make the soul the subject of "spiritual care" while the body becomes the subject of "medical care". Holistic spirituality cares for the whole person from a spiritual point of view while holistic medicine cares for the whole person from a medical point of view. There is no competition nor should there be any antipathy between these two approaches. Both are complementary. Both are necessary for the welfare of the person.

We still have a long way to go before the spiritual dimension is fully embraced by hospitals and surgeries. Despite some major developments in America Dr Harold Koenig comments on his own work in this way:

> In discussing the findings of these studies with other medical professionals, several major implications occurred to me. First, most physicians and psychologists still do not recognize the healing potential of religious faith in people's lives. Clinicians treating people in hospitals emphasize the scientific (and often the impersonal) aspects of therapy. But these same doctors, nurses, and psychologists play a role in controlling patients' access to chaplains, religious reading material and broadcasts, and hospital worship services. If health care professionals don't begin to recognize the power of religious faith to help people recover from depression, I believe a major healing resource will be wasted.[9]

Dr Elizabeth McSherry dedicated years to researching this question: Could devoting more attention to people's spiritual needs when they are ill lead to better outcomes in their physical and emotional health and thus reduce the cost of health care and make better use of increasingly scarce resources? Her research focused on the role of chaplains and the effect of a chaplain's visit to a sick person in hospital. She encouraged the chaplains to make their own "spiritual diagnosis" and to assess the spiritual needs of the patients. This kind of pastoral visit would take time. The patient would have as long as he or she needed to talk about life, about anxieties and worries, concerns about the past or guilt that were carried over into the present. It would be an "in-depth" pastoral visit.

Dr McSherry found compelling evidence that good pastoral care along the lines she was proposing enhances healing and saves a lot of money. As her team commented: "Lengths of stay in hospitals and resource utilization can be significantly lowered if the spiritual issues are adequately dealt with."[10] Professor Benson of Harvard calculates that the American health system would save a staggering "$50 billion per year" if good pastoral care was available to those in hospitals.[11] Good pastoral care could save the system from bankruptcy. That is why the big insurance companies are now taking a keen interest in pastoral care. Dr Koenig comments: "In many ways it's ironic that cost-conscious health care executives are rediscovering the connection between hospitals and the clergy, which reflects the traditional Judeo-Christian view of the bond between body and spirit."[12]

A landmark research project on the relationship between religious involvement and long life was carried out in California with a group of 5,286 people aged between twenty-one and sixty-five by Dr William Stawbridge and his colleagues. The aim of the research was to discover if there is any long-term connection between attendance at religious services and a reduced death risk. And, if there was a connection, how could it be explained? In reporting the results of this research Dr Koenig writes:

> One of the researchers' most significant findings when they measured mortality in the entire group was that the hazard of dying during the years of the study for the frequent religious attenders was 36 per cent less than for people who

attended services less than once a week. Careful analysis of the data showed that some of this protection probably derived from the close family ties and friendships these people enjoyed and from their better health practices. Even when these important factors were considered, however, the more religiously involved people still had an overall 23 per cent reduced risk of dying between 1965 and 1994.[13]

The researchers took into account the fact that those who regularly attend religious services have a much broader and more intimate group of friends; they are normally very committed to loving community and engaged in all kinds of services within the community; they normally drink less alcohol, probably refuse to take any kind of illicit drugs and try to give up smoking; they don't engage in promiscuous sexual behaviour and most often are faithful to one partner. All this amounts to quite a healthy lifestyle. Koenig comments: "Although these elements may combine to help preserve health and extend life, they account for only about one-third of the relationship between religious attendance and survival."[14]

What can explain the difference in longevity that the Stawbridge research showed? Koenig tentatively reaches this conclusion:

> Perhaps the inner peace and deep personal faith combined with the bond of loving concern within a congregation that many religiously active people experience might underpin much of this intriguing suggestion of faith's healing power. The subtle effect of faith on long-term stress reduction, which often leads to better physical health, may be a powerful factor, accounting for some of this otherwise unexplained longevity.[15]

The message coming from medical research today is that spirituality and religious practice are good for your health and that good pastoral care will save the health system a lot of money. It is not any kind of religious practice but "intrinsic religiosity" that hastens healing and recovery and protects especially against depression in the elderly. Dr Koenig's research team studied the effects of "intrinsic religiosity", when religion and faith are the primary motivating force in a person's life, on the recovery from depression. They were able to conclude thus:

> After examining twenty-eight different variables, including quality of life, family history of psychiatric disorders, severity of physical illness and change in severity over time, social support, and treatment with antidepressants, we learned that intrinsic religiosity was one of the most important factors in speed of recovery. The higher the person's intrinsic religiosity, the faster he or she recovered from depression.[16]

Intrinsic versus Extrinsic

Research has now focused on the real difference between the healing effect of a religious faith that is extrinsic and one that is intrinsic. Extrinsic people may practise religion, but for them religion and the values and beliefs of religion have not been internalized. Religion is something they put on or off as suits their other needs, for example need for social status, self-justification, security and sociability. They "have got religion" but "religion hasn't got them". They are like the man who once said to me that he was a Catholic but he wasn't a fanatic. He went to church once a year for midnight Mass. For intrinsic persons religion holds the meaning of their existence. They have internalized their beliefs; their faith is the deepest thing about them; all their ultimate securities and their very reason for living are found in their faith. This distinction between these two ways of "being religious" is fundamental and very often it was ignored in research into the relationship between faith and health. A purely extrinsic faith will not yield health benefits. Richards and Bergin comment:

> It is clear from such findings that these two ways of being religious have different implications for mental health. It is no wonder, then, that generic studies of religion that do not make such distinctions consistently yield ambiguous implications for health because they lump together different individuals under the same label of "religious".[17]

These two psychiatrists emphasize the following points about intrinsic religious faith:

(1) Religious belief gives a person a secure identity which helps the person deal with stress and uncertainties.

(2) Religious faith gives a person a real sense of purpose in life and enables the person to find meaning even in death.

(3) The positive emotions of faith and hope and optimism are fostered by ritual and forgiveness and the hope of salvation.

(4) Religious belief introduces a person into a network of believers where they have a sense of belonging to the community, a sense of family where they receive social support and have the opportunity to help others.

(5) Religious belief, through prayer and worship, gives the person a sense of communion with God and imparts inner peace.

(6) Many religious beliefs call for a lifestyle that includes self-control, taking responsibility, avoiding destructive or sinful ways.[18]

We are conscious today that not all forms of religious faith or zeal are healthy. We have witnessed the devastation of militant fundamentalism in various world religions. The 11 September 2001 attack on the World Trade Centre in New York, with its horrific loss of life, was carried out in the name of religion. Religion, then, is not a uniformly benign phenomenon. Some of the worst atrocities of human history have been perpetrated in the name of religion by religious fanatics. When we speak about the healing power of religion we have to be conscious of this dark side of religion. As Richards and Bergin comment: "Although the accumulating evidence for mental and physical health benefits of some features of religiousness and spirituality are massive, we recognise that the picture is not always positive. Clinical practitioners who are treating disturbed individuals often see some of the worst aspects of religion."[19]

The medical research which I am quoting here was all carried out after I had published the first edition of this book. We can see that there is a great change taking place in the worldview of medical scientists. Are we now ready to respond to this change and enter into a new partnership between the Church and the medical world for the promotion of the true welfare of the sick? The Catholic Church has always celebrated a sacrament for the sick, though for many centuries this sacrament was restricted to those who were in danger of death. The Church today clearly proposes two sacraments to the faithful for the healing of body, mind and spirit. In the *Catechism of the Catholic Church* we read:

> The Lord Jesus Christ, physician of our souls and bodies, who forgave the sins of the paralytic and restored him to bodily health, willed that his Church continue, in the power of the Holy Spirit, his work of healing and salvation, even among her own members. This is the purpose of the two sacraments of healing: the sacrament of Penance and the sacrament of Anointing of the Sick. [20]

The Catechism, published in 1994, says that the sacrament of penance, more popularly known as Confession, is a "sacrament of healing". Too often in all the many laudable efforts being made to make this sacrament relevant in the life of the Church today this healing dimension of the sacrament is overlooked, and sometimes totally ignored. The focus still tends to be on "the forgiveness of sin" with little or no mention of what Pope Paul VI called "the healing of the wound of sin". Sacramentally, priests who are the ministers of both these sacraments of healing, penance and the anointing of the sick, are at the forefront of the healing ministry. Psychologically and emotionally many priests are still not at ease with praying for healing. Praying for the forgiveness of sins, yes, but not for healing! The healing ministry is still not fully accepted in the Church. The different ways of praying for healing which other Christian Churches have developed and which are also highly developed within the Catholic Church rarely, if ever, feature in the formation courses of students preparing for the priesthood. We need "a radical conversion of thinking" before the healing dimension of our faith and sacraments is fully accepted.

While priests are the sacramental leaders of the healing ministry in the Church they don't have to be the ones who do all the praying for healing. In fact, the priest who is personally involved in the healing ministry usually encourages the growth of team ministry. He relies on the ministry of the laity and he encourages the development of this ministry. An Anglican priest and four of his lay ministers attended a workshop I was giving in January 2002 on the healing ministry. They were working in an inner-city parish and they were determined to bring the healing riches of Christ to the poor and the afflicted. In 1985 a Catholic bishop invited me to conduct a workshop on the healing ministry for the priests and people of his diocese. A good number of lay people turned up for the day. Only one priest attended the day. The bishop confided to me that he despaired of getting his priests interested in the healing ministry. The sad truth is that if the priest doesn't show interest he impedes the development of this ministry among the laity. He also precipitates the laity's search for a healing ministry elsewhere.

The Anglican Church published a major report on the healing ministry in 2000 entitled *A Time To Heal*.[21] This is a very comprehensive survey of the state of the healing ministry in the Anglican Church. They can report:

> We are glad to discover that almost every bishop has some involvement in the healing ministry, particularly anointing, laying on of hands and intercessory prayer as well as taking part in the annual Chrism service during Holy Week. About half of the diocesan bishops currently chair their diocesan committees involved in or relating to this ministry, which is a clear signal of the importance they attach to its place in their diocese. ...Some bishops encourage and are also involved in training conferences and annual diocesan healing days and services. A few bishops are also involved with healing organizations or a particular initiative, or hold a national post related to the healing ministry. Many diocesan advisors feel that the involvement and support of their bishops is a crucial factor in promoting this ministry within the diocese. It is also important that the media see that the bishops have a keen interest in it; this helps to show society that healing is a central part of the Church's mission.[22]

The Report, while acknowledging that in the past fifty years, since the last official Report, some very significant developments have taken place within the Anglican approach to and acceptance of the healing ministry, also says: "it is clear from our research carried out recently that there is still much to be done to establish this ministry as a part of normal, everyday life within every parish".[23] If a similar survey of the state of the healing ministry in the Catholic Church in

Britain were undertaken I doubt that it would be able to report comparable development. Despite the renewal of the liturgy and the emergence of lay ministry in the Catholic Church there has been little official support for the healing ministry. Happily thousands of devoted lay ministers bring Holy Communion to the sick and the elderly in their homes, but how many of them have been trained in any way to pray for healing with them? Could we as Catholics dream, as the Anglican Report does, of seeing "the healing ministry as part of the normal, everyday life within every parish"?

At the end of one of my courses on healing in our retreat centre, a lady said to the whole group, with great joy: "I have felt inhibited with regard to things spiritual all my life. I couldn't talk about them and I certainly couldn't spontaneously pray with anyone. Now I have discovered that I can comfortably pray for healing with others. I must now bring this back to my parish." She was a pillar of the parish with an unused gift, the gift of praying with others and ministering to their hurts and inner wounds. How would her parish receive such a message? In the Church of England Report we read this apposite observation: "while some parishes do not have a high-profile healing ministry because of the views of the priest, there are very few known cases of a parish rejecting this ministry at the request of the laity".[24] There are many thousands of lay Catholics who are gifted by the Spirit for the ministry of healing but they are not receiving any training, recognition or encouragement. Without the active involvement of the parish priest the laity will remain inhibited with regard to prayer ministry of any kind, especially healing prayer. In view of the startling developments in the medical world, carers in the Church can now enter into their ministry of healing with enthusiasm and understanding in the awareness that at least some medical experts recognize the validity of their ministry in the care of the sick. The pastoral carer does not have to be knowledgeable about medical matters but he or she must be well versed in the word of God. As Bishop Ambrose Griffiths wrote in his Foreword to the first edition of this book: "There is no question of a special technique: it is simply a matter of willingly and honestly bringing all our past hurts and resentments before Christ and asking him to heal them while giving us the power to forgive." Healing comes through the word of God and the pastoral carer should be able competently to guide the sick through the word. As Scripture says, "Your word, is a lamp to my feet and a light to my path" (Ps 119.105).

The aim of this new edition is to help readers deepen their conviction in God's healing intention and to encourage them enthusiastically to do what Jesus asks us to do, namely "live ... by every word that comes from the mouth of God" (Mt 4.3). The ministry of prayer for healing is based on this faith in the word of God, on the determination to live by the word, and on confidence in bringing the word to those who are sick. Each of us is called in some way to share in this ministry as we bring the good news of Christ to world.

In preparing this new edition I had the invaluable assistance of Sr Josephine of the Dysert Carmel, Kirkcaldy. My gratitude to her. My thanks too to Rosemary Gallagher, my editor at Redemptorist Publications. Without her encouragement this new edition would not have been prepared. A special word of thanks is due to the many people who, having read the first edition of this book, wrote to express their gratitude for the help it gave them. I have treasured their words of encouragement.

Notes

[1] Herbert Benson, *Timeless Healing: The Power and Biology of Belief,* New York: Scribner, 1996, pp. 195-217.

[2] Larry Dossey, *Reinventing Medicine: Beyond Mind-Body to a New Era of Healing,* San Francisco: Harper & Row, 1999, p. 199.

[3] Andrew Newberg and Eugence D'Aquili, *Why God Won't Go Away: Brain Science and the Biology of Belief,* New York: Ballantine Books, 2001, p. 130.

4 Ibid., p. 130.

5 Harold G. Koenig, *The Healing Power of Faith: Science Explores Medicine's Last Great Frontier,* New York: Simon and Schuster, 1999, p. 246.

6 Ibid., p. 222

7 Wilkie Au, *By Way of the Heart*, Mahwah, New Jersey: Paulist Press, 1989, p. 18.

8 *Catechism of the Catholic Church,* paragraph 365.

9 Koenig, *Healing Power of Faith,* p. 152.

10 Ibid., p. 242.

11 Benson, *Timeless Healing,* p. 224.

12 Koenig, *Healing Power of Faith,* p. 247.

13 Ibid., p. 165.

14 Ibid., p. 168.

15 Ibid., p. 168.

16 Ibid., p. 151.

17 P. Scott Richards and Allen Bergin, *A Spiritual Strategy for Counseling and Psychotherapy,* Washington DC: American Psychological Association, 1997, p. 80.

18 Ibid., p. 89.

19 Ibid., P. 87.

20 *Catechism of the Catholic Church*, para. 1421

21 *A Time To Heal*, London: Church House Publishing, 2000

22 Ibid., p. 41.

23 Ibid., p. 37.

24 Ibid., p. 37.

Foreword

There is an increasing interest in the ministry of healing, but most people still hold back because they are unsure how to begin. They have the impression that healing was only common in the early days of the Church and is now confined to "special" people. Those who hesitate will find much encouragement in this book and once they have begun they will want to read on. Father Jim McManus shares with us some of his pastoral experiences and the insights he has gained. All that he has come to understand is clearly supported by the Scriptures and the texts of the Second Vatican Council, and he helps us to see these with new eyes.

Healing was integral to Christ's ministry and was continued by the apostles as the Holy Spirit worked in them as he had in Christ. Healing spearheaded evangelization by the early Christians but when it declined after the time of Constantine the theory was propounded that it was a special gift for the beginning of the Church. Now a renewed understanding of the sacraments, and especially those of reconciliation and anointing of the sick, makes it clear that healing is a central work of the Church as it was of Christ. Nor is it limited to the ordained ministers, because we know that the Holy Spirit works in all members of the Church and Christ promised that we are to do the same works as he did himself and indeed greater works.

It is always Christ who heals and his healing involves the whole person. The fullness of life which is Christ's wish for us is only possible if we are able to accept ourselves as Christ made us and are convinced that we are truly precious in his sight. This is called healing of the self-image and is the first step towards the healing of our relationships with others through forgiveness and the healing of our memories through changing the way in which we remember the past. There is no question of a special technique: it is simply a matter of willingly and honestly bringing all our past hurts and resentments before Christ and asking him to heal them while giving us the power to forgive.

When inner healing does not take place in response to our prayer it is almost always because of a variety of barriers that we place in its way, such as lack of self-acceptance or lack of genuine repentance. In some cases, we can be held bound by the influences of evil spirits and then there is need for prayer of deliverance, which is really a command in the name of Jesus that the evil spirits should depart.

Many people think first of physical healing, but this is one of the last topics treated in this book because it is only a very small part of the total healing ministry. Indeed, it is pointed out that while someone can be healed by medical science of a serious illness and yet remain deeply embittered the physical healing brought about by Christ is always part of the total healing of the whole person. It is very often the inner spiritual healing which is the more important.

Prayer for healing with real faith can do much to enrich the celebration of the sacraments and the general ministry of Christians to one another. It was an important element in the growth of the early Church and it is urgently needed today when so many people suffer from such deep hurts. This book will convince you of its orthodoxy and give you courage to begin.

Ambrose Griffiths OSB
Bishop of Hexham and Newcastle

Introduction to the First Edition

During a parish mission, in a very large parish, I met a lady who had just recently lapsed from the practice of her faith. She was very angry. What she said to me then has remained with me ever since: "The thing that hurts me most is that I am not even missed." Nobody knew she was there, nobody knew she was not there. For the first time I got a real insight into how the faith of the individual can be at risk in a large, anonymous congregation.

This lady's bitter complaint was particularly poignant to me because I was at that time in her parish encouraging people to come back to the practice of the faith. The irony of the situation hit me between the eyes. Here I was trying to persuade her to come back to a community that did not even know she existed! I was forced to look very carefully at my own pastoral strategy. It is not sufficient to get people "into the church". The real challenge is to ensure that they arrive in the church as brothers and sisters, as God's family, as a true community.

Shortly after this experience I read a very significant report from the Vatican on why some Catholics leave the Church to join new religious movements. The Vatican had asked all the bishops of the Catholic world to investigate in their own dioceses why this was happening: what made these new religious movements so attractive? (As I write this I am very conscious of a telephone call that I had just yesterday. A friend rang me in great distress to inform me that twenty-five members of her once-thriving prayer group had all left the Church. Some of them were eucharistic ministers and readers; all of them were devout Catholics. Now they were members of a new religious group.) In that report from the Vatican, entitled *Sects or New Religious Movements?* (19 May 1986), we have a very positive analysis of this phenomenon of Catholics leaving the

Church, not because they have lost their faith but because their faith is no longer nourished by their parish. Catholics are leaving the Church, we are told, because they are looking for a warm, welcoming community, in which they are known and in which their gifts are recognized and used. They are also looking for the experience of the healing love of God, touching the deep areas of their lives where they need healing. And they are looking for simple, clear, biblical answers to the complicated questions of our times.

To meet this new challenge the Holy See calls on the Church to do two things:

1. Special attention should be paid to the experiential dimension, i.e. discovering Christ personally through prayer and dedication (e.g. the charismatic and born-again movements). Many Christians live as if they had never been born at all;

2. Special attention must be given to the healing ministry through prayer, reconciliation, fellowship and care. Our pastoral concern should not be one-dimensional. It should extend not only to the spiritual, but also to the physical, social, cultural, economic and political dimensions.[1]

The report concludes with the observation that if we meet the challenge of the sects in this way "the sects will prove to have been the greatest stimulus for the renewal of the Church".

While warning us against the dangers of a "one-dimensional ministry" the Church is emphasizing two new aspects of ministry namely "the experiential dimension" of our faith and "the healing ministry". This signals a sea change in our traditional catholic formation in the faith. When I was being trained as a young Redemptorist I got the distinct impression, from the books I was reading, that the most dangerous thing I could ever have in my whole religious life would be a religious experience and, if I ever had such a thing, I must never speak about it to anyone. Emotions had nothing to do with spiritual and religious formation.

Today the experience of God is at the very forefront of the Church's awareness of evangelization. Pope John Paul II writes: "the evangelist is a witness to the experience of God".[1] It is not enough to teach "ideas about God"; nor does it even suffice to share our deepest conviction about God. There are times when we have to share our experience of God. As Jesus said to the ex-demoniac who wanted to follow him, "Go home to your people and tell them all that the Lord in his mercy has done for you" (Mk 5.19). That is the good news. What the Lord has done for you! When you witness to that you are, in Pope John Paul's understanding of the word, an "evangelist".

In writing this book I have become acutely aware of the change that has taken place in my own attitude to ministry. Thirty years ago I would not have been able to approach any question of faith on the experiential level. My pastoral approach, while being based on theology, was dominated by the insights of pastoral psychology and sociology. I felt that if I really had a deep understanding of these sciences I would be well equipped for ministry.

My very first task as a priest was to teach moral theology in our seminary. I had studied moral theology in the Alphonsianum in Rome in the 1960s. It was a first-class institute. It prepared its students well for the task of teaching. But there was one area of the priest's life and work which it left untouched, that is the area of the priest's ministry as described by the Second Vatican Council: "Priests will acquire holiness in their own distinctive way by exercising their functions sincerely and tirelessly in the Spirit of Christ" (Decree on the Ministry and Life of Priests, para. 13).

What does it mean to minister in the Spirit? My theology did not tackle that subject. I had been taught well how to minister with theological and psychological insight. But there was no course on how to minister in the Spirit, with the discernment of the Spirit. There was no emphasis on the "experiential dimension of our faith" nor on the "healing ministry". This is not a criticism of my theological institute. It is simply the recognition that this is a relatively new emphasis in the Catholic Church. The theology of the 1960s did not deal with this emphasis; in some cases even the theology of the 1990s is not dealing with this emphasis either.

The Holy Spirit is "doing a new thing" in the Church. Pope John XXIII did not pray for "a new theology"; he prayed for "a new Pentecost". Pope Paul VI told us: "The Church needs her perennial Pentecost: she needs fire in her heart, words on her lips, prophecy in her outlook... This is what the Church needs, she needs the Holy Spirit! The Holy Spirit in us, in each of us and in all of us together, in us who are the Church."[2] And he reminded us that "We are living a privileged moment of the Spirit in the Church."[3] Pope John Paul II has continued to place the same emphasis on the Spirit. In his first encyclical he told us: "The present-day Church seems to repeat with ever greater fervour and with holy insistence: Come, Holy Spirit... This appeal to the Spirit, intended precisely to obtain the Spirit, is the answer to all the materialisms of our age."[4] There is a whole new awareness of the powerful presence of the Holy Spirit in the Church. Consequently, we can now easily talk about ministering in the Spirit and the title I am giving to this book, "Healing in the Spirit", reflects this.

In many ways this book is a personal reflection on my own transition from a ministry over-dependent on theological and psychological insights to a ministry which seeks to be totally dependent on the Holy Spirit. As Pope Paul VI so eloquently said:

> Techniques of evangelization are good, but not even the most perfect of them could replace the gentle action of the Spirit. Without the Holy Spirit, the finest preparation of the evangelist has no effect. Without him, the most convincing dialectic is powerless over the mind of man, and the most elaborate projects based on sociological or psychological data prove vain and worthless.[5]

In the first three chapters, I will outline the basic theological presuppositions of the healing ministry – the principles underlying our ministry in the Spirit. The remaining chapters show how these principles are applied in the actual ministry of healing. I try to avoid abstract discussion and illustrate the various points of teaching with examples drawn from my own pastoral experience.

In writing this book I have had the support and encouragement of many friends. My two confrères Beverly Ahearn and Tony Cassidy made many helpful suggestions. My special thanks to my editor Morag Reeve: her gentle encouragement ensured that I met the deadline.

I am especially indebted to the men and women whose stories appear in this book and in whose lives I saw the healing power of the Spirit. My thanks to each one of them, especially to Pamela, Marie and Claire who responded to my request and wrote their testimonies at short notice.

Notes

[1] *L'Osservatore Romano,* 19 May 1986 (English edition).
[2] The Mission of the Redeemer, 90.
[3] General Audience, 30 November 1972.
[4] Exhortation on Evangelization, 75.
[5] The Redeemer of Man, 8.
[6] Exhortation on Evangelization, 75.

1

Our Christian Vision of the World We Live In

When I was speaking to a lady who had been diagnosed as having cancer, and given less than a year to live by her consultant, I said to her that the Lord was very close to her throughout her long illness. She replied immediately: "That is the wonder of these past months. Christ has been so close, his peace and presence so real, that I wouldn't have missed it for anything. In fact my only big worry was in case God would withdraw this wonderful peace." Her spontaneous, faith-filled remark forced me to ask myself what kind of a perspective on life does a person have which enables her to say that she wanted this peace of Christ even more than physical health? St Paul had answered this question a long time ago: "All I want is to know Christ and the power of his resurrection and to share his sufferings by reproducing the pattern of his death" (Phil 3.10).

It struck me vividly that here is a woman who has completely integrated her faith, not only in the way she is living the Gospel in her personal life, but in the way she is viewing everything, the whole of reality, in the light of the Gospel. Paul said, "all I want is to know Christ"; she said, "I wouldn't have missed the peace and presence of Christ for anything".

Pamela (and I will return to her story in Chapter 8 of this book) had a faith vision, or a faith-inspired perspective on her life in this world. When she looked out on our beautiful world she was aware, not just of the beauty, but of the wonderful, creative love of God which brought the whole thing into existence. Most of all, she was aware that even though she was just one minute individual in this immense cosmos, God loved her with a personal and infinite love and Christ, her Redeemer, was her closest friend. Her Christian worldview made her world appear a good and a friendly place. Despite all that is wrong, despite the terrors and the tragedies, the sickness and the struggles, God loves her world so much that "he gave up his only-begotten to save it" (Jn 3.16). She would be the first to admit that her faith vision of life in this world was a comfort and a support to her in times of great suffering.

Not everyone, of course, has religious faith. Some years ago I was staying with very dear friends in Bavaria. The husband, an excellent person, is a convinced agnostic. On one occasion we began to discuss faith. I said that without my faith in the creative love of God, present and active in the world, the whole universe would be a very silent place. "That's it", he responded, "when I look at the universe I am met by utter silence." I could look out from his lounge at the beautiful Bavarian Alps, rising majestically into the sky, and be filled with awe at God's love and power. My friend would rhapsodize about the beauty of the Alps, but could not find a whisper of God in any of them. He is a very fine man, full of kindness, goodness, patience, trustfulness – full, in fact, of many of the fruits of the Spirit (Gal 5.22). But he has no faith in God and looks out on his beautiful world, enjoying his Alps, without the slightest reference to a Creator. The great German theologian Karl Rahner would have seen him as "an anonymous Christian", a man who is living the Gospel without knowing the Christ of the Gospel.

Faith Perspective

My Bavarian friend's attitude made the word of Scripture all the more forceful: "It is by faith that we understand that the universe was created by God's word, so that what can be seen was made out of what cannot be seen" (Heb 11.3). As believers, we have been gifted with this faith. We can say, "We believe in God, the Father Almighty, maker of heaven and earth and of all things, seen and unseen". Faith in God and in God's creation provides us with our perspective on the world. Our world is not a closed system, originating through some inexplicable "big bang". Our world originates in God's creative love.

Secularist Perspective

The predominant mind-set in our society, however, is far removed from the faith vision. It is secularist: that is, the underlying conviction is atheistic, or at least agnostic. The predominant conviction is that the only world that counts is this visible, tangible world, and the only time that matters is the here and now, not some hereafter. And yet, despite this secularist outlook, the yearning for spirituality, for the transcendent, is very active. Indeed, Pope John Paul points to this yearning as one of the signs of the times in our new millennium. He writes:

> Is it not one of the "signs of the times" that in today's world, despite widespread secularisation, there is a widespread demand for spirituality, a demand which expresses itself in large part as a renewed need for prayer?[1]

Even when there is no direct denial of a spiritual world there is the prevailing conviction that we can safely ignore those "spiritual realities" which are grounded in religious faith. Humans do not need a God to be good, or spiritual, or to find complete fulfilment. The inhabitants of this worldview would find it very hard to cope with Pamela. They would, no doubt, respect her, but explain away her deep religious conviction and inner peace as some form of delusion. The world we live in, and not the faith we profess, can easily form our worldview. Even though we look on ourselves as believers we can look out on the world with the perspective of the unbeliever.

Creation

We cannot think seriously about our world if we ignore the question of creation. Did God create our universe or did it just happen? The answer to that question separates believers from unbelievers. Believers will unhesitatingly affirm belief in creation. Belief in creation, however, does not automatically guarantee a faith perspective on the world. Sometimes we seek to combine personal faith in creation with a perspective on life which basically ignores or denies the implications of such faith. Our life can become compartmentalized. Sunday is for an hour's religion; the rest of the week is "for business as usual".

Developing the perspective of faith, however, enables us to discover the loving design of God at the very heart of our history. I discovered this graphically in a man who belonged to that group of prisoners who became known as "The Birmingham Six". He was an innocent man and suffered greatly at the time of his arrest. He claimed that a confession was beaten out of him. During a weekend retreat, which I was giving in his prison, he was so cheerful that I asked him how he could keep his spirits up despite all he had suffered. He responded very seriously: "I can thank God for every day I have been in this prison. Before I was picked up I lived an aimless life. I had no knowledge of God. In this prison I have got to know the Lord in my life and I can live as a free man. When I was outside I imagined I was free. But I wasn't free at all."

In prison this man had developed a faith perspective on life. Far from inducing a timid, quiescent attitude, his new-found faith fired him with a fearless courage. He challenged each and every injustice in the prison and he fought unflinchingly for the ultimate dismissal of all the charges against him and the others who were wrongly sentenced with him.

The God we worship is not only the God of the sanctuary – of peaceful prayer and liturgy; he is the God of the prison, with his people in their isolation and pain. He is also the God of "the marketplace", at the heart of our economic and political life. God is not confined to the churches we build for him.

Years ago I gave a weekend retreat to a group of laymen, basing my reflections on this sentence from the Vatican Council: "It is the special vocation of the laity to seek the kingdom of God by engaging in temporal affairs and directing them according to God's will."[2] The message was that they must find God at work, not just in church. The following year some of that group were back on retreat. One man told me with great joy that he was now finding God everywhere – in his factory, in his social club, and most of all in his garden. He received the grace to do everything "in the name of Our Lord Jesus Christ". His whole prayer life was transformed and he lived daily in the presence of God. This gave him a faith perspective on life.

A faith perspective on life is such a blessing when a loved one is dying. I experienced this very vividly when my mother died at the age of eighty-seven. For two weeks the whole family gathered to be with her during her last days. Two of us sat with her in her hospital room around the clock. Each evening the rest of us gathered in the home of my brother or sister for Mass and I brought Holy Communion to my mother and those with her. Although she was unable to speak, she was able to receive with great devotion.

Two days before she died she seemed to be in a coma. Her eyes remained tightly closed and her teeth firmly clenched all day. The nurses failed to get her mouth open. I brought Communion that evening as usual, thinking to myself that only my brother and sister would receive. As soon as I entered her room my mother opened her eyes. Her eyes, filled with a most brilliant light, followed me as I crossed the room and left the Blessed Sacrament on the table. I said to my sister, "She has recognized the presence of the Lord." Then I proceeded with the prayers before Holy Communion.

My mother's eyes were still glowing and fixed on me. I was feeling very elated at the wonderful expression on her face, but sad that she would not be able to open her mouth to receive. The moment I held up the sacred host and said, "Mum, the Body of Christ", her mouth opened wide and she received. Immediately, her eyes closed and her teeth clenched again and she seemed to be back in her coma.

We were privileged to see this moment of transfiguration in her life. The presence of Our Lord in the Blessed Sacrament called her out of a deep coma and filled her with a radiant peace. It was a wonderful confirmation of her faith perspective on life.

In our faith perspective we are aware of God's creative love at the heart of our universe (the mystery of creation); we are aware that we rejected this love and sinned (the mystery of the Fall); we are aware that God did not leave us in our sin but came to rescue us through Christ (the mystery of our redemption); we are aware that Christ suffered and died for us and rose to the new life of the resurrection in order to fill us with the Holy Spirit (the mystery of the Church); we are aware that we are invited to live the life of the Spirit here and now in this life (the mystery of eternal life). Our vision of life in this world is formed and informed by these deep convictions of faith.

Image of God
God revealed to us the mystery of our own being when he declared that we are made in his "image and likeness" (Gen 1.26). We are not simply "rational animals", as the ancient Greeks thought; we are separated from the animal kingdom by more than rationality. Nor are we simply some kind of evolutionary phenomenon of nature,

as the secularist view would have it. Within that evolutionary process we have been uniquely created by God. God's Spirit teaches us to acknowledge this uniqueness of our creation with this prayer:

> For it was you who created my being,
> knit me together in my mother's womb.
> I thank you for the wonder of my being,
> for the wonders of your creation. (Ps 139.13-14)

Because we are uniquely created and loved by God we must thank God for the "wonder of our being", the wonder of ourselves. I will have much more to say about this prayer when we discuss inner healing chapter four.

"Seen and Unseen"

We believe that God created an unseen world, an intangible world, which is intimately involved in the drama of our salvation. By very definition the scientist cannot observe or analyse this unseen world. But thousands of believing scientists have found the inspiration for their exploration of the observable world in their faith in the unseen wonders of God's creation.

When I gave a parish mission in Holy Spirit Parish in Huntsville, Alabama, the parish priest boasted that there were more scientists per square foot in his parish than in "any place else in the world!" Huntsville is one of the homes of Nasa, which has developed the entire American space programme. I was deeply edified and thrilled by the deep faith which I found in so many of those great scientists. At the 5.30 morning Mass throughout the week many of them were there; they were back again for the mission service in the evening. In this parish I discovered, in flesh and blood, what the Church has always taught, namely that there is no conflict between faith and science. Those scientists making that mission, preached by my confrere Charles Corrigan and myself, were at the forefront of the scientific exploration of space, but each of them personally was deeply engaged in the exploration of his or her own relationship with God. They had a faith perspective on their life and work. Their enthusiasm for journeying into space was fired by their spiritual journey into the mystery of God. The fact that they could not observe or measure the "unseen world" was no reason for denying its existence. They believed God's word.

We know of the existence of this spiritual world because we are told about it in the Bible and the Church professes faith in it.

Angelic World

As well as the physical universe which we can see and observe, we believe in the reality of an angelic world, which we do not see. Many people have had experiences of this angelic world. I consider an experience which I had, while driving my car, an "angel experience". I had filled the car with petrol before starting off on a long journey. After driving for thirty minutes, just before I was about to join the motorway, I heard a loud, clear voice which said, with a note of alarm "check the oil". It was so clear and authoritative that I pulled into the service station which I was about to pass. I checked the oil. The dipstick came up dry! Had I joined the motorway I would have been in big trouble with the engine of the car.

You may have had similar experiences of an invisible, helping and protecting hand in times of danger. Some people would, of course, explain the "voice" I heard in psychological rather than angelic terms. Since I believe in my guardian angel I find it much more satisfactory to accept that my angel was at hand to help me.

The Church formally professes faith in angels. The Fourth Lateran Council decreed:

> There is but one true God... The one principle of all things, creator of all things visible and invisible, spiritual and bodily, who, by his almighty power, from the beginning of time has made out of nothing each of these two creatures, spiritual and bodily, that is angelic and belonging to this world.

The First Vatican Council renewed this declaration of faith in the same terms. The new *Catechism of the Catholic Church*, formulating the Church's faith for our time, re-emphasizes the teaching of the Lateran Council and states that "The existence of the spiritual, non-corporeal beings that Sacred Scripture usually calls 'angels' is a truth of faith" (para. 328). We profess faith not just in the creation of the physical universe that we see around us. We affirm faith in the invisible world that we cannot see. Without revelation from God we cannot know of the reality of this invisible universe. It would be pointless to ask even the greatest scientist whether such a world exists. It is not a question of science, or philosophy, or even of theology. It is a question of faith. The Catholic Church teaches that there is a spiritual world, inhabited by spiritual beings, pure spirits. The Church also believes that some of these pure spirits sinned and became evil spirits, or devils.

Angels

In its liturgy the Church seeks to instil in us a deep awareness that we do not stand alone before God. We are united with the holy angels of God. There is an ancient maxim in theology which states that "the way the Church prays manifests what the Church believes" (in its Latin form, *lex orandi, lex credendi*). If we apply this maxim to the Church's prayers about the holy angels there can be little doubt that the Church firmly believes that these holy angels exist. They exist to help us. As Scripture says, "Are not all angels spirits in the divine service, sent to serve for the sake of those who are to inherit salvation?" (Heb 1.14).

In the Fourth Eucharistic Prayer we say:

> Countless hosts of angels stand before you to do your will;
> they look upon your splendour
> and praise you, night and day.
> United with them,
> and in the name of every creature under heaven,
> we too praise your glory as we say:
> Holy, holy, holy...

In the Preface of every Mass we remind ourselves that we "join our voices with all the choirs of angels". In the Mass we also acknowledge that the angels, like us, praise God through Christ. We pray in the Preface of the Angels:

> Through Christ our Lord
> the great army of angels rejoices in your glory.
> In adoration and joy
> we make their hymn of praise our own.

Not only do we renew our faith in the holy angels each time we celebrate Mass, but the Church also celebrates the feast of the archangels, Sts Michael, Gabriel and Raphael (29 September), and the feast of the Guardian Angels (2 October). In the prayers for these feasts we thank God for the protection of the holy angels:

> God our Father,
> in your loving providence
> you send your holy angels to watch over us.
> Hear our prayers,
> defend us always by their protection
> and let us share your life with them for ever.
> *(Opening Prayer from Mass of the Guardian Angels)*

Since God in his 'loving providence' sends us his angels we, who are always in need of his protection, should surely joyfully accept them. We celebrate the feast of the Guardian Angels because Jesus tells us that God has given to each person a special angel (Mt 18.10). I am conscious that some fine biblical scholars would not accept what I have just written about angels. The Scriptures, they say, have something very important to say about God and about God's relationship with the world: angels are images or myths or human concepts constructed to convey some truth about God.

While biblical scholars provide the members of the Church with a great service, it is the Church itself which teaches its members the faith. That is why I have outlined above the official teaching of the Church on the reality of angels. About angels, we believe no more or no less than the Church proposes to our belief. As Cardinal Newman expressed it so beautifully: "And I hold in veneration, for the love of him alone, holy Church as his creation and her teaching as his own."

Fallen Angels

The Church clearly teaches the existence of good spirits. But the Church also believes that, in a most mysterious way, some of these good spirits rebelled against God and lost his grace. They became devils. They used their freedom to sin and rebel against God.

No aspect of Catholic teaching is more offensive to some people than this "belief in devils". We do not, of course, "believe in the devil". That would be an erroneous way of speaking. Satanists "believe in the devil". They put their trust in him. They worship him. We believe that the word of God tells us about the reality of Satan and his evil spirits. Our faith is in God and in God's revelation. Pope Paul VI reaffirmed the Church's teaching on the reality of this world of fallen angels: "Evil is not merely a lack of something, but an effective agent, a living, spiritual being, perverted and perverting. A terrible reality". And he went on to state that "It is contrary to the teaching of the Bible and the Church to refuse to recognize the existence of such a reality."[3] Pope John Paul II, in his encyclical on the Holy Spirit, restates the teaching of the Second Vatican Council and says that Christ "was crucified and rose again to break the stranglehold of *personified Evil*".[4] There is no doubt about the official teaching of the Catholic Church: the devil and his evil spirits exist. They are hostile to God, enemies of the children of God, implacably opposed to the Kingdom of God.

The reality of evil lies within the experience of each one of us. There are two kinds of evil. The evil of sin, for which we humans are responsible, an evil which manifests itself in exploitation, hatred, murder and violence of all kind. And there is the evil which Pope John Paul II calls "personified evil", for which we are not responsible, but which constantly seeks to control us through our own sinfulness. The evil which we see around us cannot simply be reduced to the sum of human wickedness. At the same time, it cannot be explained simply in terms of "personified evil". Hence the great need for discernment. As Heinrich Schlier wrote:

> Frequently there is only a thin dividing line between good and bad spirits, and it is only a clear and sharp insight which God grants us that can tell the difference, and dispel the mist which the evil spirit deliberately creates. Where this gift is lacking, there is danger that we may suspect the dark influence of the devil to be at work everywhere, so that we may never recognize him when he is really there; or we may minimize his presence and fail to see him even when he is in our midst.[5]

In a well-known passage C.S. Lewis makes the same point:

> There are two equal and opposite errors into which our race can fall about the devils. One is to disbelieve in their existence. The other is to believe, and to feel an excessive and unhealthy interest in them. They themselves are equally pleased by both errors and hail a materialist or a magician with the same delight.[6]

Behind every evil in the world there lurks the reality of the demonic, an invisible, spiritual world, where the powers of darkness are at work. Sin in the human heart, whether it be pride, greed or lust, can open the door to demonic influence. As Pope Paul said: "This question of the devil and the influence he can exert on individuals as well as communities, whole societies and events, is an important chapter of Catholic doctrine which is given little attention today, though it should be studied again."[7]

Yet we have to acknowledge that not all Christian theologians and biblical scholars accept the Church's teaching. The view expressed by Francis Wright Beare in his commentary on Matthew's Gospel is quite typical:

> There is no doubt that the early Christians, like most of the Jews of the time, believed that there was such a mighty spirit of evil; nor can we question the fact that Jesus himself shared these beliefs. None the less, we must recognise that this is a mythical conception that has lost appeal to the minds of men; we cannot ourselves accept it without falling victims to superstition.[8]

This reduction of evil spirits to mythical language has to be challenged not simply at the biblical and theological level, but also at the pastoral level. Exorcism is needed today just as it was needed at the time of Christ. John Richards has a timely warning for scholars:

> Few theologians appear to have taken any great pains to find out what has or has not happened in history, or have taken account of anthropology, parapsychology, psychic research, comparative religion or spiritualism, before assessing what needs to be demythologized. In my own limited reading of these subjects, I have encountered present-day equivalents of so many New Testament phenomena that I would strongly discourage scholars and preachers from too great an enthusiasm for dismissing as unhistorical what they have not themselves experienced.[9]

Even some pastors or theologians can accept the modern secularist outlook and assert that since they have never personally experienced people under the influence of evil spirits, such spirits do not exist. Maybe the reason why they have never had this experience is because they are convinced that evil spirits cannot exist!

Biblical theories have pastoral implications. Demythologizing the New Testament teaching on the reality of evil spirits declares the ministry of exorcism, in all its forms, obsolete. The discernment of the need for exorcism belongs to pastors and ministers rather than academics and theologians. Academic theories on demythologization have little relevance for those who have been involved in witchcraft and satanist worship or for the victims of such occult practices.

Experience of the Occult Powers

A friend of mine once rang me in a state of great anxiety and fear. She asked me if I could come and celebrate Mass and bless her flat because, she said, "I am convinced there is some kind of evil presence in my flat and it is due to a prisoner who has taken a hatred to me." This particular prisoner was serving a life sentence for a murder committed during some kind of satanic ritual. He became a Catholic in prison and Marie was his godmother. He had become very jealous and possessive of her and when she did not give him all her time, but talked to the other men, he vowed to harm her. She described what happened:

> He was very upset and angry. He asked me if I would like a "little visitor" in my flat. Days went by and I began to feel very nervous and anxious about everything. I could not understand what was happening to me. I became afraid of going out, of driving or just meeting people. My flat became very strange and cold at times. I felt there was something or someone there. I began to lose my appetite and lose weight. My sleep was also disturbed. I woke up nearly every night for several weeks in a massive sweat with a feeling of something horrifying in the room.

> I continued to go into the prison and I especially hated going in on a Sunday because I knew this prisoner would sit in the front row and leer at me. His face grew more and more awful with horrible sores all over. He told many of the officers and inmates that I was a witch and that he had made a doll of me and was sticking pins in various parts.

> One particular night I was so scared that I got the holy water and sprinkled the room and it seemed as if something left and I felt better. I did this every night for a while but I was still feeling scared and as if there was a kind of malign presence in the flat. I started to pray the rosary and kept the rosary in my hand while sleeping, with the holy water near at hand.

> A priest friend of mine came and said Mass and blessed the flat. Everything seemed better but there was still something underneath that I could not put my finger on. This priest said I should also pray for the prisoner, which I found

difficult to do after all the suffering he caused me. At any rate I did pray for him and almost immediately all the fear, anxiety and terror left me and I became my old self again.

When I returned to the prison on the next Sunday the prisoner was still sitting on the front row – but this time he had his head down. After Mass he approached me and fell on his knees before me, begging for pardon. He said that something had happened to him during the week. All anger and hatred had left him. He admitted that he wanted to cause me harm – actual death if possible.

The occult powers which that prisoner was trying to use against Marie were defeated by the symbols of faith, namely holy water and the rosary, and by the Mass and her prayers for his salvation. She was not set free by reducing everything to an over-active imagination. She wrote: "I told the chaplain about my concerns and about how I was feeling and my problems in the flat and how I was having problems sleeping. I was told that if I took a good glass of whisky before I went to bed I would be fine. Needless to say it didn't work".

Some years ago my confrère Fr Ahearn and I were asked by a religious sister to help four sixth-form girls. They had been experimenting with the ouija board. When we arrived at the convent we found these young ladies in the grip of fear: they could not sleep, eat, or concentrate on their work. They had been contaminated by some kind of evil beyond their understanding. They knew, in their own experience, the cruel reality of the demonic. They also experienced the power of Jesus setting them free when I uttered a silent prayer.

For years I discussed the ministry of exorcism with an eminent theologian who is now deceased. He was firmly convinced that the devil does not exist. His pastoral view of things was this: no devil, no evil spirits, no ministry of exorcism or deliverance. Yet he always loved to hear stories of deliverance. He was fascinated by how those four girls were set free from contamination with the ouija board by a silent prayer of command in the name of Jesus. I would put this question to him: How can a silent prayer of command in the name of Jesus set people free from such contamination and from burdens which they have carried for years and from which no therapy could release them? He always refused to answer. Since the prayer was in silence he could not explain the fruit of the prayer in psychological terms. It could not be autosuggestion! He would always smile when I would say, "Don't you see that the real explanation is that something heard and something obeyed?" The evil spirit heard the silent command in the name of Jesus and departed.

Pastoral theology and practice must be based not on biblical or theological theories but on pastoral experience. Good theology is never just a reflection on the experience of the People of God. The experience is that people are not freed from molestation by evil spirits through biblical theories, which deny their existence, but through ministry in the name of Jesus, which casts them out. We will consider this in more detail in a later chapter.

Catholic Worldview
The Catholic worldview includes, then, not just the visible world, which we can see, but the angelic world, which we cannot see. At the heart of the Catholic worldview, the Catholic *Weltanschauung,* there is an orientation to the supernatural, the spiritual, the unseen, the intangible. Our vision is informed by our faith in Christ, seated at the right hand of God in glory.

Pamela had that vision. Because of her experience of Christ she could say, despite all her suffering, "I wouldn't have missed it for anything." The prisoner who was unjustly sentenced has that faith vision. He could say "I can thank God for every day I have spent in this prison." Marie has that vision. When she was attacked by evil powers she used active prayer and her faith in the power of God, symbolized in holy water and the rosary, to resist.

Each of us should be seeking daily to form this faith vision for ourselves. Within this worldview it is logical for the Church to honour the holy angels and, at the same time, to warn us to be on our guard against the wiles of the devil. In the Lord's Prayer, Jesus himself taught us to pray to the Father to be "delivered from the evil one". Since the Church believes strongly in the reality of this spiritual world, where the holy angels exist to worship God and serve humankind, and also where the devil and his evil spirits exist to oppose God and destroy humankind, the Vatican Council had no hesitation in declaring that "The whole of human history has been the story of dour combat with the powers of evil, stretching, as our Lord tells us, from the very dawn of history until the last day."[10]

Since earliest times, the Church has urged its members to be aware of this spiritual struggle at the heart of history and to use the spiritual weapons of prayer, fasting and intercession to defend themselves against all attacks of the devil. The Church too has never hesitated to use the ministry of exorcism to expel evil spirits from people whom they have possessed.

At the same time, the Church has never exaggerated the reality of the demonic. The devil is a creature. He is a fallen angel. As such, the devil is limited in both his knowledge and power. The Church has always assured its members that those who live in the light of God, those who pray to the Father and turn to Christ for the forgiveness of their sins, have no need to fear "the powers of darkness". When we walk in the light, the darkness cannot touch us. That is why, although we believe that the devil exists, we live our lives, under the Lordship of Jesus, undisturbed by his existence. In fact, as Dom Benedict Heron has rightly observed, "Satan and the demons have more to fear from us than we have from them, if we keep our eyes fixed on Jesus and if his praises are on our lips and in our hearts."[11]

Notes

[1] At the Beginning of the New Millennium, 33.

[2] Constitution on the Church, 31.

[3] Pope Paul VI, *L'Osservatore Romano*, 23 November 1972.

[4] Encyclical on Holy Spirit, 29; cf. Constitution on the Church in the Modern World, 2.

[5] Cited in Graham Twelftree, *Christ Triumphant: Exorcism Then and Now,* London: Hodder & Stoughton, 1985, p. 157.

[6] C.S. Lewis, *The Screwtape Letters,* London: Bles, 1944, p. 9.

[7] *L'Osservatore Romano*, 23 November 1972.

[8] Francis Wright Beare, *The Gospel according to Matthew,* Oxford: Blackwell, 1981, p. 107.

[9] John Richards, *But Deliver Us From Evil,* London: Darton, Longman & Todd, 1974, p. 32.

[10] Constitution on the Church in the Modern World, 37.

[11] Dom Benedict Heron OSB, *Praying for Healing,* London: Darton, Longman & Todd, 1989, p. 96.

2

Christ and the Spiritual World

The promise of God to humankind is summed up in the words of the prophet Joel: "Afterward I will pour out my spirit on all flesh" (Joel 2.28). God, who is spirit, wants to dwell with us, who are flesh.

God promises us his Spirit to overcome the devastation and alienation caused by sin. When God created us he declared that we were "very good" (Gen 1.31). God loved us. Yet, despite God's great love for us we sinned. We cut ourselves off from God. Through our sin we entered into a state of alienation: alienation from God, from neighbour, from ourselves.

In our sinful state of alienation we had lost our way and lost our capacity for life with God. God, however, had compassion on us. Because he loved us "with an everlasting love", his love could not change. Despite our sin and alienation we remained "precious in his sight" (Isa 43.4). God determined to redeem us. We would have to be created afresh, born again. God planned a new creation in which we would be reborn of the Holy Spirit. God announced this new creation, this new birth in the Holy Spirit, through the prophets. In the prophecy of Jeremiah God promised to enter into a new covenant with his people: "This is the covenant that I will make with the house of Israel after those days, says the Lord: I will put my law, within them, and I will write it on their hearts; and I will be their God, and they shall be my people" (Jer 31.33). In the prophecy of Ezekiel God promised a new heart: "A new heart I will give you and a new spirit I will put within you..." (Ezek 36.26). In the prophecy of Joel, God summed up all his promises in these words: "Afterward I will pour out my spirit on all flesh" (Joel 2.28).

God's intention, then is clear. He wants to overcome the alienation caused by sin. He wants to unite himself to us, in his Spirit, so that we may live through his Spirit. God fulfilled all these promises through Our Lord Jesus Christ. St Paul writes: "For in him every one of God's promises is a 'Yes'" (2 Cor 1.20). It was not only through Jesus, but also in Jesus that God fulfilled his promises.

Jesus: Man of the Spirit

Through his incarnation the Son of God became one of us. He took on our human nature, with all its weakness. Jesus' first claim about himself was that God had fulfilled his promise and poured out his Spirit. He read the passage "The spirit of the Lord is upon me, because he has anointed me" (Lk 4.18) and he told his hearers: "Today this scripture has been fulfilled in your hearing" (Lk 4.21). Jesus presents himself to the people as the one on whom the Father has poured out the Spirit. Jesus is flesh, like us. The Father's promise was to "pour out the Spirit on all flesh". Jesus is now claiming that the Father has fulfilled that promise. At the very conception of Jesus the Holy Spirit was active. The angel announced to Mary: "The Holy Spirit will come upon you, and the power of the Most High will overshadow you" (Lk 1.35).

Jesus was conceived through the power of the Holy Spirit. God the Son entered our history; he became a human being like us; he was born, through the power of the Holy Spirit, of Mary his virgin mother. He was endowed with all our human faculties: a human mind and heart, human emotions and intelligence, human hopes and desires. Jesus, by divine nature the Son of God, by human nature the Son of Mary, is for ever totally identified with our sinful human history and destiny.

At the very conception of Jesus, then, there was an outpouring of the Holy Spirit. God's promise to "pour out the Spirit" was being fulfilled.

This mystery of the incarnation is at the very centre of our Christian faith. We believe not just that Jesus was the greatest prophet and spiritual leader of all times. We believe that while being fully human, sharing in all our human weakness, Jesus was the Son of the living God. Although Jesus became like us in all things but sin, there can never be another human being like him in his unique oneness with God.

Once when I was giving a retreat to a community of religious men an elderly brother asked to see me. He said to me, "You are talking a great deal about the Father of Jesus. That was St Joseph, wasn't it?" This was a totally unexpected comment. I tried rather clumsily to explain that St Joseph was the foster father of Jesus. Jesus was conceived by the Holy Spirit. God was his Father. And so, I said, we believe that Jesus is God, equal to the Father. He looked at me for some time, absorbing what I was trying to say. Then he replied, "Well, I still think the Father is a superior being."

The fact that this man lived his life in a religious community and, through no apparent fault of his own, did not accurately profess the faith of the Church in the divinity of Jesus Christ puzzled me. He was probably never asked in his whole life: "Do you believe that Jesus is the Son of God equal to the Father?" It would have been presumed that as a practising Catholic, wanting to dedicate his life to God, he would believe in the incarnation. Could it be that there are others who while professing faith do not really believe in the total reality of the mystery of the incarnation? That in every way Jesus is human, and in every way he is divine? I was forced to examine my own faith.

We are not expected to understand how Jesus, whom we can see as a baby in his mother's arms, could at the same time be God. Even more challenging, we cannot see how Jesus, dying on the cross, could at the same time be the living God. If we could see his divinity there would be no need for faith. Indeed, Jesus himself tells us that "no one has seen God". We cannot see God with our human eyes. We cannot, therefore, see God in Jesus with our human eyes. His divinity, hidden in his humanity, is disclosed only to the eye of faith. Faith in Christ's divinity is at the heart of all Christian faith. "The divinity of Christ is the cornerstone holding up the two mysteries of the Trinity and the Incarnation. Take this stone away and the whole structure of Christian faith collapses."[1] We believe that God, the creator of the universe, is so present in our human history that Jesus of Nazareth, born of the virgin Mary, is at the same time the eternal Son of God. The world into which Jesus was born was created through him and for him. As Scripture says: "He is the image of the invisible God, the firstborn of all creation; for in him all things in heaven and on earth were created, things visible and invisible, whether thrones or dominions or rulers or powers – all things have been created through him and for him" (Col 1.15-16). Everything that is, including ourselves, was created in and through and for Christ. Sin usurped the very purpose of our creation. Sin denied that we belonged to Christ. That is why Christ himself came to save us.

In his Millennium letter Pope John Paul reflects on the mystery of the incarnation in this way:

> "The Word became flesh" (Jn 1:14). This striking formulation by John of the mystery of Christ is confirmed by the entire New Testament. The Apostle Paul takes this same approach when he affirms that the Son of God was born "of the race of David, according to the flesh" (cf. Rom 1:3; cf. 9:5). If today, because of the rationalism found in so much of contemporary culture, it is above all faith in the divinity of Christ that has become problematic, in other historical and cultural contexts there was a tendency to diminish and do away with the historical concreteness of Jesus' humanity. But for the Church's faith it is essential

and indispensable to affirm that the Word truly "became flesh" and took on *every aspect of humanity*, except sin (cf. Heb 4:15). From this perspective, the incarnation is truly a *kenosis* – a "self-emptying" – on the part of the Son of God of that glory which is his from all eternity (Phil 2:6-8; cf. 1 Pt 3:18). [2]

The Promise Fulfilled:
Jesus Baptized in the Holy Spirit

St Luke describes the scene well: "Now when all the people were baptized, and when Jesus also had been baptized and was praying the heaven was opened, and the Holy Spirit descended upon him in bodily form, like a dove. And a voice came from heaven, 'You are my Son, the Beloved; with you I am well pleased'" (Lk 3.21-22). God the Father had promised to pour out his Spirit. He has now fulfilled his promise. He has poured out the Spirit on Jesus.

Jesus was not baptized with the Spirit through the baptism of John the Baptist. Jesus was at prayer when the Father baptized him in the Holy Spirit. John is the witness. He tells us: "I saw the Spirit descending from heaven like a dove, and it remained on him. I myself did not know him, but the one who sent me to baptize with water said to me, 'He on whom you see the Spirit descend and remain is the one who baptizes with the Holy Spirit'" (Jn 1.32-33). While Jesus was at prayer, John saw the Spirit descend. The outpouring of the Spirit was the Father's response to the prayer of Jesus.

It is surely fitting that on the occasion of the fulfilment of God's promise to pour out his Spirit we should get a glimpse of the mystery not only of the person of Jesus but also of the God of the promise. The voice acknowledges Jesus with the words "You are my Son, the Beloved"; it not only confirms the testimony of John the Baptist but also reveals another more profound dimension of the truth about Jesus of Nazareth as Messiah. It is this: *the Messiah is the beloved*

Son of the Father. This solemn exaltation cannot be reduced to the messianic mission of the Servant of the Lord.[3] There has been a lot of discussion about Jesus' knowledge of himself and about how he "increased in wisdom, stature, and in favour with God and people" (Lk. 2.52). Pope John Paul writes:

> However valid it may be to maintain that, because of the human condition which made him grow "in wisdom and stature, and in favour with God and man", his human awareness of his own mystery would also have progressed to its fullest expression in his glorified humanity, there is no doubt that already in his historical existence Jesus was aware of his identity as the Son of God. John emphasises this to the point of affirming that it was ultimately because of this awareness that Jesus was rejected and condemned: they sought to kill him "because he not only broke the sabbath but also called God his Father, making himself equal with God".[4]

The "voice" says to Jesus not only that he is "Son", but also that he is "the Beloved". Jesus is being told by the Father what kind of Messiah he is going to be. He would not be the political, triumphant Messiah whom the people were expecting, the Messiah who would liberate them from the oppression of the Romans. He would be the suffering Servant of the Lord, the Messiah in whom the servant prophecies of Isaiah would be fulfilled: "Here is my servant, whom I uphold, my chosen, in whom my soul delights; I have put my spirit upon him; he will bring forth justice to the nations" (Isa 42.1). Jesus knew the prophecies. He knew that he was chosen to be the "suffering servant", the "man of sorrows and familiar with suffering" (Isa 53.3). He will be able to say to the two disciples on the road to Emmaus, after his resurrection, "'Oh, how foolish you are, and how slow of heart to believe all that the prophets have declared! Was it not necessary that the Messiah should suffer these things and then enter into his glory?" Then beginning with Moses and all the prophets, he interpreted to them the things about himself in all the scriptures" (Lk 24.25-27).

When the Father pours out the Holy Spirit he declares that Jesus is at one and the same time the eternal Son and the promised Messiah. "Messiah" means "the anointed one". Jesus was anointed with the Holy Spirit. As St Peter said, "God anointed Jesus of Nazareth with the Holy Spirit and with power... he went about doing good and healing all who were oppressed by the devil, for God was with him" (Acts 10.38).

Jesus: Led by the Spirit

Jesus' immediate response to this gift of the Father is to allow the Spirit to guide him. St Luke says "he was led by the Spirit". This is a new experience of the Spirit for Jesus. The experience of being "filled with the Spirit" was the gift of the Father; the experience of being "led by the Spirit" was Jesus' response to the gift. Having received the gift of the Spirit from the Father, Jesus had to decide not just what to do next; rather, he had to decide what he would allow the Spirit to do. And he allowed the Spirit to lead him.

The Spirit would lead Jesus only into doing the will of the Father. In preparation for doing the Father's will, in the work of our salvation, the Spirit led Jesus into the wilderness where he fasted and prayed for forty days and where he encountered the evil spirit, Satan. It is surely significant that when the Holy Spirit had been poured out the evil spirit manifested himself. The evil spirit had to investigate who Jesus was. He had his suspicions, but he was not sure: "If you are the Son of God, command these stones to become loaves of bread" (Mt 4.2).

Commenting on the temptations of Jesus, I. Howard Marshall writes: "Jesus certainly took for granted the reality of Satan."[5] Montague in his commentary on the temptations of Jesus as recorded in Mark's Gospel writes:

> Mark is not concerned, as are Matthew and Luke, with the specific temptations but with the fact that the entire period is one of conflict, and the adversary is Satan. By introducing this protagonist, Mark informs us from the very beginning that Jesus' ministry will be a wrestling not with flesh and blood but with principalities and powers (cf. Eph 6.12). Jesus' conflict with Satan does not end in the desert; it only begins there. In his public ministry he will confront Satan in those possessed (1.23; 5.2; 7.25; 9.17 etc.), in the testing questions of his opponents (8.11; 10.2; 12.15) and even in the blind resistance of his own disciples (8.33). Satan is the strong man, but Jesus has come as the stronger one to bind him (1.7; 3.27). If we would understand Jesus as Mark understands him, we must accept this role of the demonic antagonism throughout the gospel.[6]

In his own experience of temptation, Jesus knew the reality of the demonic; in his experience of exorcism he saw the victory of God's Kingdom over the power of evil; in his death and resurrection he would know the full victory over evil. As St John said: "The Son of God was revealed for this purpose, to destroy the works of the devil" (1 Jn 3.8).

Jesus: In the Power of the Spirit

Jesus is prepared to face this demonic antagonism because, as St Luke says, he returned from the Jordan "with the power of the Spirit in him". Jesus begins his ministry of proclaiming the Gospel in the power of the Spirit.

In becoming man Jesus entered into our human weakness. In that state of weakness he was always in union with his Father, always doing what pleased the Father, but he was not ready for his ministry. He had to wait until he was empowered by the Spirit. The Gospel, as St Luke reminds us, consists of "all that Jesus did and taught" (Acts 1.1). The Gospel consists of both the works and the words of Jesus. For a long time I tended to separate the works of Jesus from the words of Jesus. I would then present the Gospel entirely in terms of the words. In this way, while remaining very faithful to the words, I really overlooked his works. In a sense I "verbalized" the Gospel. Jesus exercised a fourfold ministry of preaching and teaching, of healing the sick and exorcizing evil spirits. If we separate what Jesus did from what he taught we can easily reduce his ministry to preaching and teaching and ignore his ministry of healing and exorcism. We might even be saying to ourselves, as I think I was, that whereas his teaching and preaching are relevant for every age, his healings and exorcisms were peculiar to Jesus himself and relevant for his own age and culture alone.

Yet Jesus himself promised that his disciples would continue to do the same works that he himself did. He performed all his works through the power of the Holy Spirit. Since he was giving the same Spirit to his disciples he expected them to do the same works. We have to see the relationship between Jesus' ministry and the power of the Spirit. Our very faith in his divine Sonship may incline us to ascribe what Jesus did to his divinity. For many years I think that was what I was doing.

In fact, I used the miracles of Jesus to prove that he was divine. Since, in my perception, the miracles proved that he was divine, I was never able to take this promise seriously: "Very truly, I tell you, the one who believes in me will also do the works that I do and, in fact, will do greater works than these, because I am going to the Father" (Jn 14.12). How could I do the same works that Jesus did?

It was like a new revelation to me when I saw, for the first time, that the Holy Spirit was the source of Christ's ministry. I was so accustomed to thinking that Jesus worked through his own divine power that I had not noticed that it was through the power of the Spirit that Jesus was exercising his ministry. I was in danger of missing an essential aspect of the incarnation: "[He] emptied himself, taking the form of a slave, being born in human likeness" (Phil 2.7). My friend on retreat, whom I mentioned above, found it hard to accept that Jesus was really divine; I was in danger of unconsciously not believing that he was really human, sharing fully in our weak human nature.

Jesus specifically identifies the Holy Spirit as the source of his power of exorcism. The Pharisees accused him of exorcizing evil spirits through the power of Beelzebub. In defence of his ministry Jesus says: "But if it is by the Spirit of God that I cast out demons, then the kingdom of God has come to you" (Mt 12.28).

The sign of the presence of the Kingdom, which Jesus is proclaiming, is what the Holy Spirit is doing through him. James Dunn comments:

> The eschatological kingdom was present for Jesus because the eschatological Spirit was present in and through him. In other words, it was not so much a case of "Where I am there is the kingdom", as "Where the Spirit is there is the kingdom". It was the manifestation of the power of God which was the sign of the kingdom.[7]

St Luke recounts the controversy over exorcism in the context of the Lord's teaching on prayer. Jesus has taught the disciples the Lord's Prayer and has encouraged them to ask the Father for what they need. "So I say to you, ask, and it will be given you; search, and you will find; knock, and the door will be opened for you." He concludes this great exhortation on asking with the words: "If you then, who are evil, know how to give good gifts to your children, how much more will the heavenly Father give the Holy Spirit to those who ask him" (Lk 11.13). In the very next sentence Luke says: "He was casting out a demon that was mute". John P. Kealy writes: "Consideration of the gift of the Holy Spirit (God's kingdom in action) leads Luke to consider the opposing spirits and the temptation of Jesus to perform a sign."[8]

Jesus, empowered by the Spirit, proclaims the Kingdom of God. To the poor, he preaches good news from God; when he encounters evil spirits, he casts them out; sick people who come to him are healed. He sent his disciples forth to do as he was doing:

> After this the Lord appointed seventy-two others and sent them on ahead of him in pairs to every town and place where he himself intended to go. He said to them… "Whenever you enter a town and its people welcome you, eat what is set before you; cure the sick who are there, and say to them, The kingdom of God has come near to you'" (Lk 10.1,8-9).

When the disciples returned from this mission and were recounting to Jesus all that they had accomplished in his name ("even the devils submit to us when we use your name"), Jesus had a wonderful experience of the Spirit:

> At that same hour Jesus rejoiced in the Holy Spirit and said: "I thank you, Father, Lord of heaven and earth, because you have hidden these things from the wise and the intelligent and have revealed them to infants… All things have been handed over to me by my Father; and no one knows who the Son is except the Father, or who the Father is except the Son and anyone to whom the Son chooses to reveal him" (Lk 10.21-22).

Jesus rejoices in the Spirit because he can reveal the Father to "mere children", to his disciples. Pope John Paul II writes:

> The union of Christ with the Holy Spirit, a union of which he is perfectly aware, is expressed in that "rejoicing", which in a certain way renders "perceptible" its hidden source. Thus there is a particular manifestation and rejoicing which is proper to the Son of Man, the Christ-Messiah, whose humanity belongs to the person of the Son of God, substantially one with the Holy Spirit in divinity.[9]

In his whole being Christ was filled with the Holy Spirit; in all his ministry he was empowered by the Spirit; in his labours for the Kingdom of God he rejoiced in the Spirit.

The Spirit of God, who was so active in Christ throughout his public ministry of preaching the Gospel, was not absent from his great work through which he redeemed us, namely, his death on the cross. Scripture tells us that "Christ... through the eternal Spirit offered himself without blemish to God" (Heb 9.14).

Christ's death was life-giving for us, because Christ died through the power of the Holy Spirit. Through that same Holy Spirit, who is "the Lord, the giver of life", Christ was raised into the new life of the resurrection. Filled with the new life of the resurrection, by the power of the Holy Spirit, Jesus came to his disciples in the upper room on Easter Sunday evening and greeted them with the words "Peace be with you". Then, he said to them, "'As the Father has sent me, so I send you.' When he had said this, he breathed on them and said to them, 'Receive the Holy Spirit. If you forgive the sins of any, they are forgiven; if you retain the sins of any, they are retained'" (Jn 20.22-23).

Jesus gives to his disciples the very same gift which he himself had received from the Father. He says "receive the gift of the Holy Spirit". He empowers them with the same power with which he had been empowered by the Father, the power of the Spirit. He entrusts to them the same mission which he himself had received from the Father, the mission of preaching the Gospel. What Jesus did through the power of the Spirit, while he walked this earth, he will continue to do through his disciples because his disciples will have his Spirit. In the Fourth Eucharistic Prayer the Church sums up everything I have been trying to say in this chapter:

> And that we might live no longer for ourselves but for him, he sent the Holy Spirit from you, Father, as his first gift to those who believe, *to complete his work on earth* and bring us the fullness of grace.

In Jesus we see all the promises of God our Father fulfilled: the Spirit is poured out; the new covenant is established; our sins are forgiven; we are reconciled with our Father; the Gospel of reconciliation is preached to the ends of the earth. All these promises are fulfilled because Jesus, the man filled with the Spirit, says to his disciples in every age: "Receive the Holy Spirit"! Live through my Spirit; be empowered by my Spirit; work through my Spirit. The wonder of our salvation is that Jesus shares fully with us that Holy Spirit whom he received from God his Father. As St John exclaimed, "From his fullness we have all received, grace upon grace"[10] (Jn 1.16).

Notes

[1] R. Cantalamessa, *Jesus Christ the Holy One of God,* Slough: St Pauls, 1991, p. 127.

[2] At the Beginning of the New Millennium, 22.

[3] Pope John Paul II, Encyclical on Holy Spirit, 19.

[4] At the Beginning of the New Millennium, 24.

[5] I. Howard Marshall, *The Gospel of Luke,* Exeter: Paternoster Press, 1978, p. 168.

[6] George Montague, *Mark,* Ann Arbor, MI: Servant Books, 1981, p. 177.

[7] James Dunn, *Jesus and the Spirit,* Philadelphia: Westminster, 1979, p. 48.

[8] John P. Kealy, *Luke's Gospel Today,* New Jersey: Dimension Books, 1979, p. 286.

[9] Encyclical on Holy Spirit, 21.

3

Jesus: Our Intercessor at the Right Hand of the Father

In one of the penitential rites of the Mass we say to Christ: "You plead for us at the right hand of the Father: Lord, have mercy ." This prayer of the Mass focuses on Christ's role as our intercessor. As Scripture says, "he is able for all time to save those who approach God through him, since he always lives to make intercession for them" (Heb 7.25).

We put our faith and trust in the risen Christ, now seated at the right hand of the Father in glory, interceding for us. As Pope John Paul says:

> Jesus is "the new man" (cf. Eph 4:24; Col 3:10) who calls redeemed humanity to share in his divine life. The mystery of the Incarnation lays the foundations for an anthropology which, reaching beyond its own limitations and contradictions, moves towards God himself, indeed towards the goal of "divinisation". This occurs through the grafting of the redeemed on to Christ and their admission into the intimacy of the Trinitarian life. The Fathers have laid great stress on this soteriological dimension of the mystery of the Incarnation: it is only because the Son of God truly became man that man, in him and through him, can truly become a child of God.[1]

We are destined for "divinisation", for an everlasting life with God. We are being transformed through the Spirit, as St Paul says, into the very likeness of Christ (2 Cor 3:18). This transformation is the work of the Spirit. It is this faith in this transformation which underlines our self-acceptance and self-esteem.

Jesus' Prayer for Another Advocate

The whole object of Christ's intercession with the Father is the outpouring of the Spirit. He promised his disciples: "I will ask the Father, and he will give you another Advocate, to be with you for ever. This is the Spirit of truth, whom the world cannot receive, because it neither sees him nor knows him. You know him, because he abides with you, and he will be in you" (Jn 14.16-17). In response to this intercession of Jesus, the Father sent the other Advocate. He poured out his Spirit on the disciples. This is the mystery of Pentecost, the mystery of the Church.

The Second Vatican Council has made it very clear that the Church is established by Christ when the Spirit is poured out: "By communicating his Spirit, Christ mystically constitutes as his body his brothers and sisters who are called together from every nation."[2]

> Rising from the dead, he sent his life-giving Spirit upon his disciples and through him set up his body which is the church as the universal sacrament of salvation.[3]

> After being lifted up on the cross and glorified, the Lord Jesus poured forth the Spirit whom he had promised, and through whom he has called and gathered together the people of the New Covenant.[4]

The Council teaches that the Church is the direct result of Christ's action of sending his Spirit. For a long time, I think, my view of the origin of the Church took this form: Jesus established his Church while he was on earth; he then sent his Spirit to sanctify and guide the Church.

I believed that the Spirit was in the Church. I did not, however, realize that it was the Spirit himself who created the Church. I think this was because I had failed to grasp the ongoing relationship between Jesus and the Spirit. I did not see the outpouring of the Spirit on Jesus as the fulfilment of the Father's promise. As a consequence I did not focus on Jesus as the man of the Spirit, the man filled with the Spirit and empowered for his ministry by the Spirit. My focus was on the divinity of Christ.

Jesus shares with us what he received from his Father. Jesus was anointed with the fullness of the Spirit by the Father. He shares that Spirit with us. Indeed, someone has aptly defined the Church in this way: "the community of those who share in the anointing of the Anointed One". Jesus cannot share with us the unique union with God whereby he and the Father are one. We call that union the "hypostatic union" –unique to Jesus and incommunicable to us. He can communicate to us what he received from the Father, namely the Holy Spirit. This communication of the Spirit, this imparting of the Spirit, is the creation of the Church.

The Church comes into being through Christ's intercession: "I will ask the Father and he will give you another Paraclete" (Jn 14.16). St John describes in detail how this gift of the other Paraclete was given:

> When it was evening on that day, the first day of the week, and the doors of the house where the disciples had met were locked for fear of the Jews, Jesus came and stood among them and said, "Peace be with you." After he said this, he showed them his hands and his side. Then the disciples rejoiced when they saw the Lord. Jesus said to them again, "Peace be with you. As the Father has sent me, so I send you." When he had said this, he breathed on them and said to them: "Receive the Holy Spirit" (Jn 20.19-22).

Reflecting on this passage, Pope John Paul writes:

> The Risen Christ, as it were beginning a new creation, "brings" to the Apostles the Holy Spirit. He brings him at the price of his own "departure": he gives them this Spirit as it were through the wounds of his crucifixion: "He showed them his hands and his side". It is in the power of this crucifixion that he says to them: "Receive the Holy Spirit."[5]

Jesus, the suffering Servant of the Lord, pleads for us through his passion and death. As the prophet foretold: "By his sufferings shall my servant justify many, taking their faults on himself...and praying all the time for sinners" (Isa 53.11-12). Through this powerful intercession, Christ won for us our salvation, the gift of the Holy Spirit.

With the coming of the Spirit the era of the Church began. As Pope John Paul said, "The time of the Church began at the moment when the promises and predictions that so explicitly refer to the Counsellor, the Spirit of truth, began to be fulfilled in complete power and clarity upon the Apostles, thus determining the birth of the Church."[6]

St Matthew gives us a different insight into the mystery of the Church. Jesus says to his disciples: "Go therefore and make disciples of all nations, baptising them in the name of the Father and of the Son and of the Holy Spirit, and teaching them to obey everything that I have commanded you. And remember I am with you always, to the end of the age" (Mt 28.19-20). St Matthew does not record the fact that Jesus either asks the Father for the Spirit or imparts it to the disciples. George Montague explains why:

> The reason appears to be that Matthew considers the resurrection and glorification of Jesus to be his entering, not heaven, but the church as an abiding presence. He is the

promised Immanuel (1.23) whose final words to the church are: "I am with you all days, even to the consummation of the world" (28.20). That means, though that the Spirit which the Father places upon Jesus (3.11; 12.28) rests upon the church which is one with him. The church has the Spirit, then, not because Jesus left the Spirit as his replacement until he returns (the view of Luke and John) or because at some moment during his ministry or after the resurrection he specifically conveyed the Spirit to the Church, but rather because, remaining with the church, Jesus baptises with the Spirit through sharing his own baptism with the disciples of all ages. Jesus does not give the Spirit to the church but rather receives it for the church. Whence the intimate and necessary identification of Christian baptism with his.[7]

The Spirit is given in response to Jesus' prayer: Jesus prayed at the Jordan and the Spirit was given to himself; he asked the Father again and the Spirit was given to us. Jesus knows the power of intercession. Jesus also knows the power of the Spirit. He told his disciples: "You will receive power when the Holy Spirit has come upon you; and then you will be my witnesses in Jerusalem, in all Judea and Samaria, and to the ends of the earth" (Acts 1.8). He knew the power of the Spirit in his own life. He wants his disciples to know that same power. Indeed, in their joy and enthusiasm after the resurrection he had to warn them not to begin their proclamation of the Gospel without that power: "Stay here in the city until you have been clothed with power from on high" (Luke 24.49).

Jesus is interceding not just for the Spirit of truth, who will guide his disciples throughout the ages, but for the Spirit of empowerment. He knows our weakness: he experienced the fragility of his own first disciples. They all deserted him. Yet Jesus had such confidence in the transforming presence of the Holy Spirit that he assured his weak and vacillating followers that they would be empowered for their mission, and that they would bring the Gospel to the ends of the earth.

Jesus' confidence in the Spirit was not disappointed. No sooner had the Spirit come upon them than the disciples began preaching the Gospel. On Pentecost day itself the preaching of Peter converted three thousand men and women! Jesus promised his disciples: "Very truly, I tell you, the one who believes in me will also do the works that I do and, in fact, will do greater works than these, because I am going to the Father" (Jn 14.12). We see this promise fulfilled in the ministry of Peter, who immediately after Pentecost began doing the works Jesus did: preaching the Gospel; healing the sick; casting out evil spirits; even raising the dead to life. St Luke describes the enthusiasm and the miracles in Jerusalem in this way:

> Now many signs and wonders were done among the people through the apostles... they even carried out the sick into the streets, and laid them on cots and mats, in order that Peter's shadow might fall on some of them as he came by. A great number of people would also gather from the towns around Jerusalem, bringing the sick and those tormented by unclean spirits, and they were all cured" (Acts 5.12-16).

Stephen, the first martyr, "full of grace and power, did great wonders and signs among the people" (Acts 6.8), while St Paul tells us how he brought the Gospel to the Thessalonians: "We know, brothers and sisters beloved by God, that he has chosen you, because our message of the gospel came to you not in word only, but also in power and in the Holy Spirit and with full conviction" (1 Thess 1.4). And writing to the Romans Paul is able to say: "In Christ Jesus, then, I have reason to boast of my work for God. For I will not venture to speak of anything except what Christ has accomplished through me to win obedience from the Gentiles, by word and deed, by the power of signs and wonders, by the power of the Spirit of God" (Rom 15.17-19).

Wherever we follow the footsteps of the apostles and the early disciples of Christ we find the Lord's promise fulfilled. They are doing the same work that he did. They are doing even greater works because now Jesus is at the right hand of the Father and is present in all his power with them.

Jesus had promised that he would ask the Father for the Spirit. He promised that the disciples would receive power when the Spirit came. And they did! Power to preach; power to heal; power to cast out evil spirits. We have to see that whole exciting beginning of the Church, as described by St Luke in Acts, as the answer to Christ's intercession. Or we can see the disciples' powerful ministry through the eyes of St Mark:

> So then the Lord Jesus, after he had spoken to them, was taken up into heaven and sat down at the right hand of God. And they went out and proclaimed the good news everywhere, while the Lord worked with them and confirmed the message by the signs that accompanied it (Mk 16.19-20).

"The Lord worked with them": that is the essence of Christian ministry. St Matthew has the same emphasis as St Mark: "remember I am with you always to the end of the age" (Mt 28.20). The disciple is never alone. The Lord is working with him or her in every situation. And just as the Lord himself worked through the power of the Holy Spirit so he is enabling his disciples today to work through that same power.

The manifestation of the power of the Spirit, through works of healing and deliverance from evil spirits, did not cease with the death of the last apostle. We find the same striking manifestation of the power of the Spirit in the early centuries of the history of the Church. Before we look at some of the witnesses from these early centuries, let us digress a little and reflect on the sanctifying role of the Spirit.

The Sanctifying Role of the Spirit

The primary role of the Holy Spirit is the sanctification of God's people. The Spirit dwells in the heart of each one of us. This abiding presence of the Spirit is given for our rebirth as God's children. As St Paul said, "And because you are children, God has sent the Spirit of his Son into our hearts crying, 'Abba! Father!'" (Gal 4.6). By sending us the Spirit, Jesus not only created the Church but, through the Spirit in our hearts, God established his new covenant with us. That word "covenant" is not an easy word to understand or explain. For years I tried to preach about it. I would try to explain that a covenant was like a pact, or an agreement, made, not between equals but between two unequals. For example, a king could enter into an agreement with one of his subjects. Being king he did not have to enter any agreement. But once he entered into an agreement, that agreement would be a covenant between him and his subject and he would have to honour it. The marvel of a covenant between God and us is that God honours his covenant: he is, as it were, bound by it.

I had a very objective or intellectual understanding of covenant. Then one day in 1968, when I was teaching moral theology in our seminary, I came across the teaching of St Thomas Aquinas. St Thomas was not talking about pacts or agreements. He wrote: "The New Covenant consists in the inpouring of the Holy Spirit",[8] and in another commentary he said: "As the Holy Spirit works in us charity which is the fullness of the Law, he himself is the New Covenant."[9]

For days I pondered those texts. How did we lose sight of them? If St Thomas, who is recognized as the greatest theologian in the history of the Church, was teaching in the thirteenth century that "the Holy Spirit is the New Covenant", why did we not receive that teaching in our catechism? I began to say to myself, "the covenant is not just some kind of objective pact or agreement; the covenant is a person, the divine person of the Holy Spirit!"

We call ourselves "the people of the New Covenant". But should we not personalize covenant, as St Thomas did, and call ourselves "the people of the Holy Spirit"? The Second Vatican Council speaks of "the priests of the New Covenant": should priests not personalize this for themselves and see themselves as Christ's priests of the Holy Spirit? And if we are priests of the Holy Spirit should we not live and work through the Spirit?

Whatever your vocation in the Church, married or single, religious, laity or priest, you are a person of the New Covenant. You are a person of the Holy Spirit. Therefore, you live and work in and through the Spirit. We receive this sanctifying gift of the Spirit as a totally unmerited grace of God. Jesus intercedes for us and the Father gives us the Spirit. God wants to form us in the perfect "image of his Son" (Rom 8.29). He wants to reproduce in us that same life in the Spirit which Jesus had, because he loves us "just as he loved Jesus". As people of the New Covenant, people of the Holy Spirit, God wants our life in the Spirit to be patterned on Christ's life in the Spirit. It took me a very long time before I could really accept with my heart this amazing good news that what God did in Jesus, through the Spirit, he wants to do in us through the same Spirit.

St Luke highlights the pattern of Christ's relationship with the Spirit in this way:

- *Jesus was filled with the Spirit.* That was God the Father's gift to him. He gives that same gift to us.

- *Jesus was led by the Spirit.* That was Jesus' response to the gift of God's Spirit. He surrendered, so that he could be led. If we wish to be led by the Spirit we must surrender just as Jesus did. His prayer of surrender "not my will, but thine be done" must become our prayer.

- *Jesus was empowered by the Spirit.* In his human weakness the power of the Spirit is present   so that he can do the works his Father gives him to do. We too in our weakness must do God's work. We receive the same empowerment of the Holy Spirit.

There is a great difference between "doing God's work" and "working for God". The empowerment of the Spirit is for doing God's work. Therefore at the heart of our ministry there must always be a prayerful and listening reference to God: does God want me to do this? Is this good work, which I am proposing to do, God's will, or is it just my holy will? There is no empowerment of the Spirit for us to do our holy will!

Sometimes, I feel, we tackle good works, plan great apostolic projects, without enquiring whether God wants us to do such a work at all. Then we storm heaven for God's blessing on a project which God may never have wanted in the first place! If we are working "in union with the Holy Spirit" we must surely always ask him, before we begin any work, whether our proposed project is really what God wants us to do. That is what we mean by discernment of God's will. It requires great detachment, prayer and self-denial. If our project is God's will, we will have the power of the Spirit for its accomplishment; if it is not God's will, the Holy Spirit will not empower us for its accomplishment.

We must never take the sanctifying gift of the Spirit in our hearts for granted. We must constantly cultivate the heart through prayer, contemplation, silence and faithful action. Pope Paul VI had a timely reflection. He said:

The Holy Spirit's presence in individual souls can diminish or be missing entirely. This is why the word of God is preached and the sacraments of grace are distributed; this is why people pray and why each individual tries to merit the great "Gift of God", the Holy Spirit, for himself and for the whole Church.[10]

Empowering Presence of the Spirit

The Spirit also dwells in our hearts for the sake of others. We are witnesses to the risen Christ, servants of the Kingdom of God. Just as Jesus, in the state of human weakness, did not proclaim the Gospel and witness to the Kingdom before he was empowered by the Holy Spirit, so we cannot witness to the Kingdom before we receive that same empowerment. That is why Jesus told his first disciples not to leave Jerusalem "until you are clothed with power from on high".

This empowerment is not for our sanctification, but for our mission. For our sanctification we need the indwelling presence of the Holy Spirit in our hearts; for our mission we need the power of the Holy Spirit in our ministry. We call the empowering presence of the Holy Spirit in our lives "charismatic grace". Sanctifying grace is given to us by the Spirit for our personal union with God; charismatic grace is given to us by the same Spirit for our mission or ministry in the Church.

Jesus promises us both the sanctifying and the empowering presence of the Spirit. It is true to say that for a long time the Church has been so concerned about the sanctifying presence of the Spirit that it has tended to neglect the empowering presence of the Spirit. Indeed, one could argue the case that for many centuries we have not really expected the Spirit to empower us with those charismatic graces with which he empowered the first Christians.

For years I led Christian communities in the Easter Vigil. When I proclaimed the words "Jesus Christ, the same yesterday, today, and for ever" (Heb 13.8) the question would always come to my mind: if this is true, why is Jesus not doing the same things today as he did among his first followers? I would answer myself in this way: Jesus is forgiving sins and sanctifying people today and that is the real work of salvation. That was my way of avoiding the challenge of the Easter proclamation. Jesus Christ is the same for us as he was for the first followers in Jerusalem. He is present to us with the same divine compassion and mercy. He wants us to have the same experience of his forgiving and healing presence as Peter and Paul had.

We have, however, "over-spiritualized" the work of Christ. We began to see his work in terms of the "salvation of the soul" and not in terms of the "salvation of the whole person". This aberration may have been due to the inculturation of the Gospel in the dominant culture of the Roman Empire. This culture was dominated by Platonic philosophy.

Plato died four hundred years before Christ. For Plato the human person is a composite of body and soul. The soul is immortal and the body is mortal. The early Christian apologists and theologians were able to identify with this philosophy. The human soul is immortal. Death is not the end. Christian thinkers began to teach and defend the faith through the philosophical language of their time. They became Christian Platonists. The necessary process of the inculturation of the Gospel had begun. The Church began to think and speak through the language of the people, using the ideas and the concepts and the images of the people.

Not all aspects of Plato's view of the composition of the human person were, however, compatible with the Christian vision. For Plato, the soul is in the body as in a prison. He had what we call "a dualistic view" – soul and body were at war with each other. The happiest day in the life of the soul is when the war is ended, through death, and the soul is released from the body.

Plato did not have much time for the body. It was flesh, corruptible and mortal. The soul was spiritual, incorruptible and immortal. Only the soul really mattered. Strains of dualism have survived the centuries!

If we believe that death is a happy release of the soul from the prison of the body, we may logically begin to conclude that anything which causes death, such as sickness, is a good thing. And, indeed, this attitude towards sickness developed in the Church. Sickness was even called "a time of divine visitation". Of course, if sickness is caused by God it would not be right to pray against it. We don't pray against what God is doing! Consequently, we don't pray for healing.

This new attitude to sickness had serious pastoral implications. The emphasis changed from the healing ministry to a spirituality of suffering. Sickness was a time of "divine visitation". The sick person should be encouraged to offer up the sufferings. Even the sacrament of the sick took on a new meaning. It ceased to be primarily a sacrament for those who were sick and in need of healing and became the sacrament of "the last anointing", Extreme Unction. The sick person would not receive this sacrament until the very final stages of illness. The anointing became so associated with dying that many people conceived a great fear of the sacrament. Even to this day some relatives will ask the priest not to speak to a very sick person about "the last rites"!

The whole focus was on the salvation of the soul. The healing and restoration of the body were not considered. Even though they were never explicitly denied, they were not expected. The result? We spiritualized the healing ministry of Jesus and saw it more in terms of the forgiveness of sins. Since Jesus continues to forgive sins today we were happy to accept our Easter proclamation that he is indeed the same yesterday, today and for ever. Despite the teaching of the Council of Trent, which explicitly stated that "sometimes sickness is healed" through anointing, the general faith expectation saw anointing only as the preparation for death.

Along with this over-spiritualization of the healing ministry of Jesus and the inordinate focus on "the soul' to the detriment of "the body", we had a waning of the charisms in the Church. But in the first three centuries we find the Church, in the midst of persecution, vigorous and strong in the Spirit. The gifts of the Spirit, especially the gift of healing, were prevalent. I will cite just a few witnesses from those early centuries.

Justin Martyr, a convert philosopher, writing around AD 165 to the Roman Emperor, pleading on behalf of the Christians, stated:

> For numberless demoniacs throughout the world, and in your own city, many of our Christian men exorcising them in the name of Jesus Christ… have healed and do heal, rendering helpless and driving the possessing demons out of them, though they could not be cured by all the other exorcists, and those who used incantations and drugs.

Later on in the second century Tertullian, an African lawyer, writing to the Roman Proconsul of North Africa during a period of persecution, reminded him of these facts:

> And how many men of rank have been delivered from devils, and healed of diseases! Even Severus himself, the father of Antonine [the Emperor] was graciously mindful of the Christians; for he sought out the Christian Proculus… and in gratitude for his having once cured him by anointing, he kept him in his palace till the day of his death.

In the following century the great theologian Origen, writing around the year AD 253, stated: "And the name of Jesus can still remove distractions from the minds of men, and expel demons, and also take away diseases; and produce a marvellous meekness of spirit and a complete change of character."[11]

From these three reliable witnesses we can see that in those first three centuries the promise of Christ was fulfilled. His disciples did the same works that he himself did. In fact it was by doing the works of Christ, healing the sick and casting out evil spirits that those first Christians had the opportunity to bring the good news of Christ to the pagans who were persecuting them.

I often asked myself how the Christians of those first three centuries managed to convert so many people, all over the pagan Roman Empire, despite the fact that they were an illegal body, persecuted, without any rights of assembly, and without any public means of communication. A historian of the ancient Roman Empire, Ramsey MacMullen, has studied this very question. He tries to imagine what openings the Christians had for converting pagans. He writes:

> I would choose a room of a sick person; there, a servant talking to a mistress, or one spouse to another, saying, perhaps, "Unquestionably they can help, if you believe". And I know, I have seen... they have related to me, they have books, they have a special person, a sort of officer. It is true... they can help even in great sickness. I know people who have seen or who have spoken to others who have seen. And healing is even the least that they tell. Theirs is truly a God all-powerful. He has worked a hundred wonders... So, a priest is sent for, or an exorcist; illness is healed; the household after that counts itself Christian; it is baptised; and through instruction it comes to accept the first consequence: that all other cults are false and wicked and all seeming gods, the same.[12]

In this view it was the healing ministry which spearheaded the early Church's evangelistic successes. Those early Christians set out not just to heal the sick and drive out demons in the name of Jesus. They set out to demonstrate that Jesus Christ alone was Lord and Saviour and that all the other gods of the pagans were worthless and powerless idols. St Antony the Hermit is a good example of this technique.

Antony lived in solitude in the desert for forty years. He attracted thousands of followers. Two pagan philosophers, who had lost students to Antony, went into the desert to debate with him. St Athanasius, in his life of Antony, relates what happened:

> Antony said to them "we convince because people first trust what they actually see, and then in reasoned argument" and Antony added "look now: here are some folk suffering from daimones... either cleanse these men by your logic-chopping or by any other skill or magic you wish, and calling on your idols, or, otherwise, if you can't lay down your quarrel with us and witness the power of Christ's cross". And with these words he called on Christ, sealed the sufferers with the sign of the cross twice and a third time, and straightaway the men stood forth all healed.[13]

In those early centuries, when the Church was suffering persecutions, the disciples continued to evangelize in the same way as Jesus did. They healed the sick, they cast out evil spirits, they brought people to an experience of the Lordship of Jesus. In the words of St Mark "the Lord worked with them, and confirmed the message by the signs that accompanied it" (Mk 16.20). Then the Emperor Constantine made peace with the Church in AD 313. He himself became a Christian and richly endowed the Church. The religious situation was transformed. The Church now had the protection of the mighty empire. Constantine wanted the Church and State to live and work in harmony.

Following the "peace of Constantine" a marked decline in the manifestation of the charisms of the Spirit seems to have taken place. Some began to find the reason for this decline, not in any decline of expectant faith, but in the plan of God himself. They developed the theory that God gave the gifts of the Spirit at the beginning of the Church, for the preaching of the Gospel "to the ends of the earth". In the ancient Roman world Spain was deemed to be the ends of the earth. There was a growing conviction that the Church had fulfilled its mandate to bring the Gospel to the whole world. The gifts of the Spirit, which were given for this purpose, were no longer needed and consequently God had withdrawn them!

Very few would subscribe to this theory, known as *dispensationalism,* today. Yet that theory held sway in the Church for nearly sixteen hundred years, right up to the Second Vatican Council. The Council happily restated the teaching of the Church on the role of charisms in the life of the Church and the sanctification of God's people. I will quote in full the main text:

> It is not only through the sacraments and the ministries that the Holy Spirit makes the people holy, leads them and enriches them with his virtues. Allotting his gifts "at will to each individual" (1 Cor 12.11), he also distributes special graces among the faithful of every rank. By these gifts, he makes them fit and ready to undertake various tasks and offices for the renewal and building up of the church, as it is written, "the manifestation of the Spirit is given to everyone for profit" (1 Cor 12.7). Whether these charisms be very remarkable or more simple and widely diffused, they are to be received with thanksgiving and consolation since they are primarily suited to and useful for the needs of the church.[14]

Since the Council's clear and prophetic teaching on the role of the charisms we have had the experience of "charismatic renewal in the Church". This renewal in the Spirit has brought the experience of the gifts of the Spirit, the gift of tongues, healings, deliverance, and many other gifts to millions of Christians all over the world.

We have witnessed the emergence of the lay ministries in the Church. Men and women, from all walks of life, have discovered that they have gifts of the Spirit for serving the community of the faithful.

We have also witnessed great renewal in parish life. In our parish of St Mary's, Clapham, I have observed over the past five years great renewal in the Spirit. Very many of our parishioners have become hungry for the Word of God. They meet in "cells" to share their faith, to listen to God's Word, to reach out to those who do not, as yet, believe in the Lord Jesus. They want to be evangelists of Christ. On parish missions I have met the same hunger for the Word of God, the same longing to become involved in the mission of the Church, in hundreds of men and women. With such a movement of the Spirit we must surely hope that the Church, especially in the parishes, will be renewed in our time.

Some observers often sound a pessimistic note when they look at the Church because of the diminishing numbers of vocations and the decreasing and ageing Sunday congregations. I would have to say, on the contrary, that in my experience the Church is far more alive today than in the 1950s, and 1960s, when we had much larger numbers. God is clearly renewing his Church, pouring out the gifts of the Spirit in abundance and gifting many people with new ministries.

One of the most significant gifts which the Spirit is reviving in the Church today is the gift of *inner healing*. Jesus said that he came so that we might have "Life in abundance". The gift of inner healing enables the Church to minister to the inner person, to heal the inner wounds and hurts which impede the abundant life which the Lord wants to give.

This ministry is for the whole Church. It is not restricted to priests or ordained ministers. In the next chapter we will consider inner healing as the great service which each of us can render to others, helping them into the experience of "life in abundance".

Notes

[1] At the Beginning of the New Millennium, 23.

[2] Constitution on the Church, 7.

[3] Constitution on the Church, 48.

[4] Decree on Ecumenism, 2.

[5] Encyclical on Holy Spirit, 24.

[6] Encyclical on Holy Spirit, 25.

[7] Kilian McDonnell and George Montague, *Christian Initiation and Baptism in the Holy Spirit,* Collegeville: Liturgical Press, 1991, p. 21.

[8] St Thomas Aquinas, *Heb. Cap.* 8, lect. 2.

[9] St Thomas Aquinas, *in 2 Cor. Cap.* 3, lect. 2.

[10] Cited in Edward O'Connor, *Pope Paul and the Spirit,* Notre Dame: Ave Maria Press, 1978, p. 154.

[11] For these quotations from the Early Fathers and many more similar texts see the excellent history of the healing ministry, Morton Kelsey, *Healing and Christianity,* London: SCM Press, 1973. For a very comprehensive study see the classical work by Evelyn Frost, *Christian Healing,* London: Mowbray, 1940.

[12] Ramsey MacMullen, *Christianizing the Roman Empire AD 100-400,* New Hdaven: Yale University Press, 1984, p. 41.

[13] Ibid.

[14] Constitution on the Church, 12.

4

Life in Abundance:
Christ's Promise

Speaking about his mission, Jesus said "I have come so that they may have life and have it to the full" (Jn 10.10). Fullness of life, life in abundance; that is Christ's wish for us.

The experience of this abundant life is impeded each time we fail to live by the word of God. In the hour of his temptation in the desert Jesus proclaimed that "One does not live by bread alone, but by every word that comes from the mouth of God" (Mt 4.4). Fullness of life cannot be achieved by living on riches, or power, or position. It can only be achieved by living on the word of God. Once lost, through sin or the wounds of sin, fullness of life can only be restored by that word of God.

Speaking about the centrality of his word in the life of the disciples, Jesus said: "If you make my word your home you will indeed be my disciples, you will learn the truth and the truth will make you free" (Jn 8.31-32). Most people know the phrase "the truth will make you free". Sometimes people mistakenly look to the blunt speaking of the truth as the best way of serving freedom. They miss the whole context of what Jesus said.

I remember once taking this word "the truth will make you free" very seriously. I said to myself, this is the secret of life. I want to be free. All I have to do is speak the truth and do the truth and then I will be free. I went at it with the zeal of a novice, but soon I discovered that, at least in my case, it didn't seem to work. When I spoke the truth to people, as I saw it, I didn't always set them free. And when people spoke the truth to me, as they saw it, they didn't always set me free either. In fact, very often the opposite was happening. I was finding resentments and anger coming, instead of freedom. I was saying to myself: "What does Jesus really mean? This is God's word! It should be an efficacious word". Then one day I was reading the whole passage again. I was amazed at the words I had never noticed. Jesus did not simply say "the truth will make you free". He laid down very precise conditions, which must be fulfilled, before the truth achieves the power to make us free. The first condition is this: "if you make my word your home". I had missed that. Some place must be home for mind and heart. The homeless mind would be even more distressing than the homeless body. Jesus invites us to make his word our home. Home is the place where you feel "at your ease". You can be yourself because you know who you are. Home gives you your identity as son or daughter of the house.

Jesus says that if we make his word our home we will receive a new identity: "you will be my disciples". This is the second condition, which must be fulfilled before the truth can make us free. I had missed that also. We are either disciples of Jesus or disciples of some other master. And, as Jesus himself said, "we cannot serve two masters". Pope John Paul II in his great encyclical on Christian morality describes what is involved in discipleship in this way: "it involves holding fast to the very person of Jesus, partaking of his life and destiny, sharing in his free and loving obedience to the Father. By responding in faith and following the one who is Incarnate Wisdom, the disciple of Jesus truly becomes a disciple of God (Jn 6.45)."[1] By identifying with Christ, in this total and personal way, we receive our new identity as his disciples.

The third condition which must be fulfilled before the truth has the power to make us free is this: "you will learn the truth". I had missed that also. I thought I knew the truth. The truth, which makes us free, is the truth, which we are willing to learn, as disciples, dwelling in the word of Jesus as in our home.

The truth about our life and destiny is contained in the word of Christ. The Church of Christ, "the pillar and butwork of the truth" (1 Tim 3.15), interprets his word for us. As the Second Vatican Council said, "The task of giving an authentic interpretation of the word of God, whether in its written form or in the form of tradition, has been entrusted to the living teaching office of the church alone. Its authority in this matter is exercised in the name of Jesus Christ."[2] Christ alone is our teacher. His teaching comes to us through his Church. Dwelling in Christ's word, as in our home, will always involve dwelling in the Church of Christ, his body on earth. The truth, which we will learn, dwelling in the word of Jesus, is the truth about God and about our relationship with God. That is the truth which will make us free.

As we live on every word that comes from the mouth of God we will learn the truth about ourselves and we will come into the freedom of the children of God. We live on some word about ourselves. We must choose either God's word or what Scripture calls "the destructive word" (Ps 52.4). The destructive word is the sinful word, the very opposite of the creative word. The destructive word is the lie about ourselves. If we live the lie about ourselves, instead of living the truth about ourselves, we will have no freedom or peace. Jesus compares his word, God's word, to a house. We can take up our residence in that house. There is also another word identified in Scripture where we can take up our residence. This is the "destructive word". We read "you love the destructive word" (Ps 52.4). We have, then, the image of two houses where we can make home, the house of the creative word of God or the house of the destructive word. We form our self-image in one of those houses.

Formation of Self-image
The self-image resides in our subconscious. It controls the way we feel about ourselves. We are not born with a self-image: it is formed

by the word that is spoken to us. Ultimately we have to say that the self-image is formed either by the word of God or by the destructive word.

If we have made our home in the house of the creative word of God we will have a good self-image; and as a result we will have true self-esteem. If, however, we have made our home in the house of the destructive word we will have a poor self-image and low self-esteem. We will feel bad about ourselves and, as a result, we will feel bad about others.

We use this formula: self-knowledge plus self-acceptance equals self-esteem. The key is, of course, self-knowledge. We are not born with self-knowledge. Everything we know about ourselves we have learned. The question is, can we trust the source of our self-knowledge? If our self-knowledge comes from the "destructive word", the sinful word, there will not be much truth in it. That is why it is so essential for us to make God's word the source of our self-knowledge. Our choice is quite simple. We either believe what God says to us about ourselves and grow in good self-esteem or believe the destructive, sinful word and develop poor self-esteem. God says to us that we are "precious in his sight" (Isa 43.4). If we decide to believe that we are of no significance in God's sight we have nobody to blame but ourselves for our poor self-esteem. We will return to this theme later.

Our self-image must be formed by the word of God. In every eventuality of life there is a word of God to live on. Entering into freedom, growing in our freedom, maintaining and protecting our freedom, will not happen if we do not faithfully live each day on Christ's word. As Pope John Paul said, "The Crucified Christ reveals the authentic meaning of freedom; he lives it fully in the total gift of himself and calls his disciples to share in his freedom."[3]

Inner Healing

Using the image of the house of the creative word and the house of the destructive word we can say that the ministry of inner healing consists in enabling a person to move out of the latter and take up residence in the former. The first step in inner healing is helping the person to escape from the prison of the destructive word. The person must be taught to listen to the word of God and live on it.

Inner healing can be defined in this way: An experience of the healing love of God in which the person realizes that self is lovable (healing of self-image) or that he or she is capable of loving and forgiving (healing of relationships) or that he or she can gratefully integrate some past event into the present (healing of memories).

Healing the Self-image

It is always prudent to begin a ministry of inner healing with prayer for the healing of the self-image. If the self-image is not formed by the word of God it will be deformed by the destructive word. A deformed self-image would be a great barrier to other forms of inner healing.

The first step in this ministry is the proclamation of God's word that the person is a beloved child of God. We help the person, through listening prayer, to get out of the house of the destructive word and take up residence in the house of the creative word.

If our self-image is formed in the house of the creative word of God it will correspond to how God himself sees us. We must see ourselves as God sees us. We do not have to guess at how God sees us; he himself tells us. The whole Bible is a long love letter, which God has written to us. In the very first chapter God tells us the model he had in mind when he created us: "Let us make humankind in our image, according to our likeness" (Gen 1.26). The first thing God reveals to us is that we are like God. God's image and likeness! God's creative love made us like himself. God declared that we are "very good" (Gen 1.31).

Then the mysterious reality of sin infected God's good creation. We cut ourselves off from God. Adam and his wife, we are told, "hid themselves from the presence of the Lord God among the trees of the garden" (Gen 3.8). When challenged by God, Adam said, "I heard the sound of you in the garden, and I was afraid, because I was naked; and I hid myself" (Gen 3.10). Adam had fallen from the paradise of God-consciousness into the pain of self-consciousness. In this new consciousness he rejected himself. He could no longer accept himself as he was. So he hid. He had alienated himself from God, but also he had rejected himself. He was ashamed. God came looking for him: "Where are you?" (Gen 3.9). It is always God who comes looking for us. When we sin we hide ourselves away from God. God calls to us, "Where are you?" That call of God has followed humankind down through the centuries.

God will not allow us to hide away in our shame. He wants us to live without fear in his presence. So he reassures us in our fallen state:

> Do not fear, for I have redeemed you;
> I have called you by name, you are mine...
> Because you are precious in my sight,
> and honoured, and I love you...
> Do not fear, for I am with you. (Isa 43.1,4,5)

God's redeeming love reaches its fulfilment in Christ. God became a human being like us in Christ. He entered into our weakness and sinfulness. Indeed, he took all our sinfulness on himself and redeemed us:

> All we like sheep have gone astray;,
> we have all turned to our own way,
> and the Lord has laid on him
> the iniquity of us all. (Isa 53.6)

Christ has redeemed us from our "fallen state". When we accept redemption from Christ we receive a new identity, the identity of the redeemed sons and daughters of God. It is only in Christ that we can know ourselves. This is how the Second Vatican Council expresses this truth:

> In reality it is only in the mystery of the Word made flesh that the mystery of humanity truly becomes clear. For Adam, the first man, was a type of him who was to come, Christ the Lord. Christ the new Adam, in the very revelation of the mystery of the Father and of his love, fully reveals humanity to itself and brings to light its very high calling. It is no wonder, then, that all the truths mentioned so far should find in him their source and their most perfect embodiment... by his incarnation, he, the Son of God, has in a certain way united himself with each individual.[4]

Christ unites us to himself. He has lifted us up out of our fallen self-consciousness and given us a Christ-consciousness. He has given us a new identity and has revealed to us our "very high calling". That is our true worth, the ground of our human dignity, the source of our self-esteem and no external circumstance of life can rob us of it. Now when we become aware of ourselves we can become aware of ourselves in union with Christ. We are not on our own. Christ lives in us. As the Council put it, "In reality it is only in the mystery of the Word made flesh that the mystery of humanity truly becomes clear". The mystery of yourself, your life and your destiny are only known to you in Christ.

In his first encyclical letter Pope John Paul II wrote:

> Those who wish to understand themselves thoroughly – and not just in accordance with the immediate, partial, often superficial, and even illusory standards and measures of their being – they must with all their unrest, uncertainty and even their weakness and sinfulness, with their life and death, draw near to Christ. They must, so to speak, enter into him with their own self, they must "appropriate" and assimilate the whole reality of the Incarnation and the Redemption in order to find themselves. If this profound process takes place within them, they then bear fruit not only of adoration of God but also of deep wonder at themselves.[5]

In this magnificent passage the Pope gives us the whole theology of the ministry of inner healing, namely "appropriating and assimilating the whole reality of the Incarnation and Redemption". He goes on to clarify and specify the Church's ministry in this way:

> The Church wishes to serve this single end: that each person may be able to find Christ, in order that Christ may walk with each person the path of life, with the power of the truth about man and the world that is contained in the mystery of the Incarnation and the Redemption and with the power of love that is radiated by that truth.[6]

The ministry of inner healing consists, then, in helping the person to "appropriate and assimilate the mystery of the Incarnation and the Redemption".

The healing of the self-image will begin when the person comes to the realization that he or she is united to Christ and that all the grace and merit of Christ become his or her own through faith and conversion. As St Paul said: "So if anyone is in Christ, there is a new creation: everything old has passed away; see, everything has become new! All this is from God" (2 Cor 5.17-18). The ministry of inner healing seeks to bring the person to that realization.

To sum up, the ministry begins with the word of God. The person must hear the invitation of Jesus: "if you make my word your home". Inner healing begins as the person begins to learn the truth about self, the truth that he or she is precious in God's sight. That is the word the person must live on.

Self-acceptance

Self-rejection is the first fruit of sin. Like Adam, sinners seek to hide themselves from the presence of God. They fear God, because they feel that their sin has robbed them of all dignity in the presence of God. They lose the sense of what the Second Vatican Council called "the surpassing dignity of humanity".[7] In our early development as children we learned that if we did certain things, which our parents and teachers said were good, we were good children. But if we did what they said was bad we were bad children. The difference between being a good child and being a bad child was found in behaviour. Since children naturally want to be seen as "good" by their parents and other significant people in their lives, children unconsciously begin to place conditions on their own worth. When they behave well they are good; when they please their parents they are good; when they do well at school they are good; when they are helpful around the house they are good. And when they are good they have the experience of being accepted and praised; when they are bad they have the experience of being scolded or even rejected. Children begin to learn a very negative message: their own personal worth is conditional on their being good and pleasing to others. What do children do? They set out to please. And what is the price? They themselves now place conditions on their own personal worth. They don't accept themselves unconditionally. They don't cultivate what Carl Rogers called "unconditional positive self- regard". That is the beginning of self-rejection. I can accept myself when I am meeting the expectations of others; I reject myself being a child of God. Instead, I make self-acceptance depend on how others respond to me. To return to our image of the two houses, we could say that now I am living in the house of the destructive word and have vacated the house of the creative word. When I place conditions on my own worth, no matter what those conditions are, even if they are "very holy conditions", I am on the road to self-rejection. If I say, "I could accept myself if I was really holy", I am on the road of self-rejection.

People find it very hard to pray. Even if they "says their prayers they will not feel comfortable in the divine presence.

A priest came to Hawkstone Hall, the Redemptorist International Pastoral and Renewal Centre for priests, religious and laity in Shropshire, for a private retreat while I was director.[8] His problem was that he could not pray and he wanted some help. He was a young active priest and had succeeded an old man who had been parish priest for thirty-five years. During those years the Second Vatican Council never happened in his parish! Now this young, dynamic priest takes over. He does all that a modern parish priest should be doing. The people are delighted and are singing his praises. But he himself is not praying. The praises of the people are getting to him. He is feeling a real hypocrite and is in danger of a breakdown. He arrived at Hawkstone Hall in a state of tension and confusion.

When I heard that his real problem was that he could not pray (he was saying all the prescribed prayers) I asked him to read out the first ten verses of Isaiah 43. When he came to the verse "because you are precious in my eyes" I asked him to respond. He said with great vehemence, "He is not referring to me". That was his problem with prayer: he felt that God had a very high opinion of everyone else but entertained a very low opinion of himself! He lived in self-rejection. He wasn't saying "lots of prayers" so he couldn't accept himself. His conditions for self-worth included being holy, being prayerful, and being a zealous priest. Since he didn't meet those conditions he felt he had no worth. But who imposed those "conditions of worth" on him? He did it himself!

I gave him a simple exercise. I asked him to join the course (there were around seventy priests and religious on a three-month renewal course) at the Holy Hour each evening and simply say, "Jesus, I thank you that I am precious in your Father's sight." He went down for his first Holy Hour to spend his time saying this prayer. He told me afterwards that he felt very foolish on that first evening. He would look around from time to time and see all the others lost in prayer and contemplation and there he was, wringing his hands and forcing himself to say, "Jesus, I thank you that I am precious in your Father's sight." But he persevered with the prayer. And in three days that man was so full of prayer that he couldn't stop praying. He was spending hours in the church, singing hymns all over the place, and, in general, living a whole new God experience. What had happened? He had begun to live on the word of God. He had vacated the house of the destructive word, in which he felt no good, and taken up residence in the house of the creative word, where he heard that he was precious in God's sight.

He began to accept himself. There were no "conditions of personal worth". He discovered the truth of Guardini's remark: "The act of self-acceptance is the root of all things. I must agree to be the person who I am. Agree to have the qualifications, which I have. Agree to live within the limitations set for me... The clarity and the courageousness of this acceptance is the foundation of all existence."[9] Self-acceptance is the goal of Christian existence. It is not there by birth, but by our rebirth. As St Peter said, "You have been born anew, not of perishable but of imperishable seed, through the living and enduring word of God" (1 Pet 1.23). My self-acceptance is not based on my own merits; it is based on God's word to me, on God's acceptance of me. The divine acceptance makes self-acceptance possible. It is a work of grace, the fruit of redemption. The Fellowship of Alcoholics Anonymous discovered the liberating and healing power of self-acceptance. This is how they express it:

> And acceptance is the answer to all my problems today. When I am disturbed today, it is because I find some person, place or thing, or situation – some fact of my life – unacceptable to me, and I can find no serenity until I accept that person, place, thing, or situation as being exactly the way it should be at the moment. Nothing, absolutely nothing happens in God's world by mistake. Until I could accept my alcoholism, I could not stay sober; until I accept life completely on life's terms, I cannot be happy. I need to concentrate not so much on what needs to be changed in the world as on what needs to be changed in me and in my attitudes.

The act of self-acceptance must be fortified by prayer and the determination to live on the word of God. Scripture teaches us to pray this prayer of self-acceptance:

> It was you who created my inmost self,
> who put me together in my mother's womb;
> for all these mysteries I thank you:
> for the wonder of myself, for the wonder of your works.
> (Ps 139.13-14)

We must not only pray this prayer, "I thank you for the wonder of myself", but we must live it. Inner healing comes to the self-image when we gratefully thank God each day for the wonder of ourselves. God delights in holding a dialogue with us. He says to us "you are precious in my eyes" and he awaits our reply. That word of God is an everlasting word spoken over each of us. We are already addressed by God, even before we turn to him in prayer. When we go to pray we have to respond to his word. As you come into God's presence in prayer God says to you, "you are precious in my sight". You have to respond. The Holy Spirit has given us this beautiful psalm for a fitting reply. Because we are precious in God's sight we can thank him for the wonder of ourselves! That is a very healing prayer to say. God sets no "conditions of worth". You are precious in his sight because you are his beloved.

Speaking about "appropriating and assimilating the whole reality of the Incarnation and Redemption", Pope John Paul II concluded:

> If this profound process takes place within them, they then bear fruit not only of adoration of God but also of deep wonder at himself. How precious must humankind be in the eyes of the Creator, if we "gained so great a Redeemer" and if God "gave his only Son" in order that we should not perish but have eternal life.[10]

This prayer of self-acceptance is the first step on the road to the healing of the self-image: growing in wonder at one's own dignity as a child of God. The prayer is the opposite of the sin. Sin causes alienation from self; sin fills the person with guilt and shame; sin may even instil a deep self-hatred. This prayer, on the other hand, fills the person with gratitude for God's wonderful creation. It opens the human spirit to rejoice in the Holy Spirit. It prepares the heart for a deeper, ongoing conversion. The more we fill ourselves with gratitude to God for the wonder of ourselves the more we will reject everything which is contrary to our dignity.

We cannot sustain for very long these two contrary modes of action, namely thanking God for the wonder of ourselves while at the same time attacking our own dignity by sinful behaviour. Such a way of behaving would create in us what psychologists call "cognitive dissonance', that is an emotional state when two simultaneously held attitudes or beliefs are inconsistent or when there is a conflict between belief and behaviour. The healing of the self-image comes about through creating this "cognitive dissonance". I may be feeling bad about self, feeling worthless. Then I begin to pray, "I thank you for the wonder of myself". This creates the healthy conflict between what I profess in prayer and what I feel in myself. By persevering with the prayer the bad feelings about self will begin to change. Instead of experiencing self-rejection or even self-hatred I will come into a new self-acceptance and a new gratitude for self. Those bad feelings about self are all related to those "conditions of worth" which I have established for self. In prayer, as we thank God for the wonder of ourselves we begin the healing work of getting rid of each "condition of worth". My worth depends on nothing other than the loving, creating will of God who called me to be his beloved son. Even if the whole world rejects me I believe God never will withdraw his love and his choice of me. My self-acceptance is built on this rock of faith.

The healing of the self-image is a process and it takes time. The key to this healing is listening to the word of God. If a person is not willing to listen to God's word there is no basis for healing. On the other hand, if the person is willing to listen to God's word, willing to live on his word, there is no wound in the self-image which will not be healed.

While working with a group of religious at Hawkstone I once asked the sister sitting next to me if she would be the first to introduce herself and tell the group why she had come on the course. She was seized with panic and had great difficulty in speaking. We all felt very sorry for her. After the session I talked to her about inner healing and promised her that she could be completely healed from this panic. She told me that the panic was there because when she was about twelve her teacher had made her stand before the whole class to do a sum which she didn't know. He called her a stupid girl and then got one of the boys to do the sum on the blackboard. That cruel remark robbed her of all self-confidence. She suffered intensely each time she had to speak in public; she could never read in public. Even though she was a highly qualified nurse, a ward sister, she felt totally inadequate in public.

She received the teaching on inner healing as good news. Each morning she would thank God for the wonder of herself and for all her good gifts. I asked her group to pray with her frequently, asking the Lord to take from her deep subconscious the word "stupid" and fill her whole being with the words "precious in my sight". Before the course was over she not only read during Mass but she also wrote a wonderful poem and recited it to the whole course. She was now living on the word of God, which declared that she was precious, and not on the word of the teacher, which declared that she was stupid. Her self-image had been healed and her confidence restored.

Healing of Relationships

The heartfelt prayer of Jesus at the Last Supper was for unity among his disciples: "I in them and you in me, that they may become completely one, so that the world may know that you have sent me" (Jn 17.23). Jesus prays that the unity of his disciples will mirror on earth the unity of the Trinity in heaven. Such a unity can only come from God. This divine gift of unity was given to the Church. The Second Vatican Council, quoting the great martyr St Cyprian, said the universal Church is "a people made one by the unity of the Father, the Son and the Holy Spirit".[11]

God wills that the multiplicity of our relationships is enriched with love and unity. "God is love, and those who abide in love abide in God, and God abides in them" (1 Jn 4.16). Disunity is not the hallmark of God's work. Unity is the fruit of grace and love; disunity is the bitter fruit of sin and selfishness. We have, regrettably, disunity: in the Church; in the home; in the extended family; among friends. Human relationships, the source of so much joy, when they are enriched with love and unity, become the source of bitter pain, when they are distorted through disunity and lack of love. But God heals broken relationships through the gift of forgiving love. St Peter asked Jesus about forgiveness: "'Lord, if another member of the church sins against me, how often should I forgive? As many as seven times?' Jesus said to him, 'Not seven times, but I tell you, seventy-seven times'" (Mt 18.21-22).

Jesus is saying to Peter that the quality of Christian forgiveness is unconditional. There are no limits. It is not a question of "How often must I forgive?"; rather, forgiveness itself becomes the very sign of my Christian existence. No forgiveness, no Christian life! Jesus concludes his parable of the unforgiving debtor with these words: "So my heavenly Father will also do to every one of you, if you do not forgive your brother or sister from your heart" (Mt 18.35). Forgiveness is never a question of "meeting the other person half-way", nor is it a question of forgiving "provided they don't do it again". Christian forgiveness lays down no conditions. It goes all the way, all the time.

Christian forgiveness, then, must be seen as an act of divine love. We are not capable of that kind of forgiveness by our own powers. It is Christ in us who enables us to forgive in this Christ-like way. Jesus reminded us, "without me you can do nothing". Without Christ, without the sincere desire to live the life of Christ, we cannot forgive unconditionally. But when we do forgive we become like God himself. "Be compassionate as your heavenly Father is compassionate" (Lk 6.36); compassionate forgiveness makes us like God himself. In the very act of forgiving we radiate God's image and likeness.

People frequently misunderstand the nature of forgiveness. They confuse forgiveness with condoning the wrong done or excusing the fault or crime of another. Forgiveness, in fact, is the very opposite of condoning or excusing. As C.S. Lewis wrote:

> There is all the difference in the world between forgiving and excusing. Forgiveness says, "yes, you have done this thing, but I accept your apology, I will never hold it against you and everything between us two will be exactly the same as it was before". But excusing says, "I see that you couldn't help it, or didn't mean it, you weren't really to blame". If one was not really to blame then there is nothing to forgive. In that sense forgiveness and excusing are almost opposite.[12]

When I say to someone "I forgive you" I am saying that the person has wronged me and that he or she had no excuse. But I am also saying that, because I am a child of the forgiving Father in heaven, I forgive in imitation of his forgiveness. In forgiving I become like God!

When I ask myself why God demands that we should forgive the person who wrongs us, the words of the psalm come to mind: "The Law of Yahweh is perfect, new life for the soul" (Ps 19.7). Forgiveness brings "new life for the soul" because forgiveness sets us free from those who hurt us.

Consider what happens within you when someone hurts you. You can spend the whole day thinking about the hurt. The person who hurt you can be in your thoughts night and day. You can become preoccupied with the person. Each time you think of him or her you experience the hurt afresh. Indeed, if the hurt was really deep, the person seems to have the power to haunt you. As one lady colourfully expressed it to me, "I am carrying him [her estranged husband] around in my head, rent free, twenty-four hours a day! I would love to get rid of him out of my mind." I gave her this image to work with: unforgiveness is like putting your two hands around a person's throat and holding tight. As long as you hold the person by the throat you will be seeing that person right in front of you. The only way to get rid of the person is to open your hands and let go. She wanted to let go.

Forgiveness, then, is letting go. Unforgiveness holds you in bondage to the person who has hurt you. Forgiveness breaks that bondage. Forgiveness sets you free. "The Law of Yahweh is perfect, new life for the soul." As soon as that lady entered into forgiveness she experienced a new freedom and got her estranged husband "out of her mind".

Because forgiveness is a divine gift it has the power "to bind up the brokenhearted" (Isa 61.1). When someone you have loved "breaks your heart" what can you do? From the pain of the broken heart you can seek revenge. You can curse the person and wish him or her all kinds of evil. Or you can take the path of freedom and forgive. Forgiveness is at the heart of the Gospel: it is not just one Christian attitude among many others. It sums up in itself the whole mystery of salvation. Because God has forgiven me, I can forgive others. When God forgives me, his forgiveness remains within me. It becomes the source of my power to forgive. Without God's forgiveness in my own life I am powerless to forgive others.

The person who has been deeply hurt has to hear the good news of forgiveness. The hurt can become the occasion of a whole new experience of the power of God. An example will illustrate this. During a parish mission in a certain city I was helped greatly by the lady who looked after the church. She was there before all the services to make sure that I had everything I needed. One afternoon, towards the end of the mission, I unexpectedly met her in the church. She was telling me how well the mission was going. I said to her, half jokingly, "I hope you have got the big blessing yourself." Her whole attitude changed at once and she said with an astonishing degree of sarcasm, "If you mean that business of honouring your father and mother that you were talking about last night you'd better forget it!"

I was quite taken aback. I knew she was a devout believer. Such a remark had to come from some very deep hurt within her. She saw the look of puzzlement on my face and she added, "If you came through what I came through you would not be surprised at what I have just said." I was praying hard for her because for the first time I recognized that she was in great need of help. It was, I felt, a moment of grace for her.

Reluctantly, she began to tell me her story. When she was one day old her mother put her in a cardboard box and left her on the steps of a church. It was a Saturday night, in the middle of winter. As the lady who was doing the flowers for Sunday morning came out of the church she saw the box and passed on. Then she heard a cry from the box and turned back. Inside was the little one-day-old baby, perishing with the cold. She not only saved the baby's life but she also adopted her as her own daughter. Now, years later, the lady was married herself and had a lovely family. But every time she heard the words "honour your father and your mother" she was gripped with a totally uncharacteristic hardness and coldness. "You wouldn't expect me to honour a woman like that, would you?" she challengingly said to me. I had the presence of mind to say, "No, I wouldn't, but I know God does, and if God wants you to honour your mother, God gives you the power to do so."

After talking about her experience for some time she agreed to my offer of prayer. I invited her to come to the foot of the cross and to listen to Jesus praying for those who were crucifying him. She knew the prayer well: "Father, forgive them, for they don't know what they are doing." I asked her to listen deeply to that prayer. She did.

Then I asked her if she would like Jesus to say that prayer for her mother. She replied, more or less, that Jesus could do what he liked! But she listened. Then I said to her that I would like to say the same prayer for her mother and so I began to repeat the prayer: "Father, forgive her, she doesn't know what she is doing." After a while I invited her to say the same prayer herself. At first she adamantly refused; then she began to waver, and finally she joined in the prayer, "Father, forgive her, she doesn't know what she is doing." The moment she entered into the prayer of forgiveness she received God's promise: "A new heart I will give you, and a new spirit I will put within you; and I will remove from your body the heart of stone and give you a heart of flesh. I will put my spirit within you" (Ezek 36.26-27). All the hardness and coldness were gone. She became grateful to God for her mother and she could once again live on the life-giving word of God: "honour your father and mother".

This woman had come to terms with the tragedy of her abandonment. She had previously convinced herself that the best way forward was never even to think about her mother. She presumed that God's commandment "honour your father and mother" did not apply to her. It was a new revelation to her of God's great love and forgiveness when he took away her "heart of stone" and gave her a new heart for her mother. What seemed totally impossible to her became possible in God's power.

By listening humbly to the prayer of Jesus on the cross and seeking to make that prayer her own she was, in the words of Pope John Paul II "appropriating and assimilating the whole reality of the Incarnation and Redemption" and so "she found herself". She found herself as a daughter in relation to the mother who had given her birth. And she honoured that mother in her heart. Jesus had fulfilled his promise, "I have come so that they may have life and have it to the full." This abundant life flowed through her as she opened her life to Jesus and sought from him the power to forgive. The power of God's forgiveness is available for the healing of every wounded relationship. How sad, then, when we find people nursing great inner wounds either because they do not know about the liberating power of forgiveness or because they simply refuse to turn to the Lord and ask for that power.

The message of the liberating power of forgiveness is not always welcome even in Christian circles. During a course in an ecumenical institute in the USA on "The dialogue between psychology and theology", I asked a question about forgiveness and much to my amazement the lecturer, a Christian minister, snapped at me and said, "I don't go in for cheap forgiveness!" She had been sharing a case with us. She was counselling a female lecturer on the campus who as a young girl had been brutally, sexually abused by her father for several years. She explained the various stages of the therapy and then told us that her next session would be the last one. She had said nothing about forgiveness, nor indeed any other spiritual dimension of the lady's life. It was at this point that I asked at what stage would she speak to the lady about the need to forgive her father. Not only did the lecturer express great indignation but also the whole class, all ministers in various churches, shared her anger at my question.

I responded rather heatedly myself and said that I did not speak of "cheap forgiveness"; I was referring to the forgiveness that comes through the passion and death of Christ, and that was no cheap forgiveness! She then responded to me and said, "She has nothing to forgive. Her father does not exist anymore." By this time, the whole class was very angry and the discussion had become less than rational.

Recognizing the strength of opinions on both sides the lecturer then proposed that we should devote the next period, the following week, to forgiveness. During the next session we had a reasonable discussion and sharing on forgiveness as a distinctly Christian response to those who wrong us. At the end of the term, while she was thanking us all for participating in the course, the lecturer said, "I can guarantee you, this is the only institute in the whole of the USA that has given one hour this term to forgiveness!"

She never gave me a satisfactory answer to this question: How could she, as a Christian minister, bring another Christian woman through a whole course of counselling and refuse to speak to her about the liberating power of Christian forgiveness? I am sure her counselling skills brought some relief to the woman she was helping; Christian forgiveness, however, would have given her a new heart. Forgiveness is like "laser surgery": no tumour of resentment or hatred can resist it. The minister of Christ who leads a person into forgiveness fulfils the Scripture:

> The spirit of the Lord God is upon me,
> because the Lord has anointed;
> He has sent me to bring good news to the oppressed,
> to bind up the brokenhearted. (Isa 61.1)

Forgiving Oneself

We must extend to ourselves the same forgiveness which we receive from God. I have often heard people declare: "I will never forgive myself for what I did." Isn't that a terrible thing to say to oneself? If God forgives us our sins, even our greatest sins, why shouldn't we forgive ourselves? Sin, of course, causes alienation from self. It can even instil hatred and loathing of self. Sin causes self-rejection. Therefore, any unwillingness to forgive oneself may be a sign of a deep root of self-rejection.

After I had spoken on this subject during a retreat at a top-security prison, one man came up to me and said, "I know exactly what you mean by the need to forgive yourself. I worshipped the ground my wife walked on, but I killed her. I can never forgive myself. I know God forgives me. I am getting out in a month's time. How can I forgive myself?" That man's inner world was shattered. Even though he was deeply repentant he was still living in the house of the destructive word. How could he, a wife-killer, be precious in God's sight? After what he had done, how could he ever say, "I thank you for the wonder of myself"?

Among his fellow prisoners there was the man who had been wrongly convicted of a terrible crime, whom I mentioned in chapter 1. This man, whose sentence has since been overturned by the Court of Appeal, had learned the secret of accepting himself, even in his dreadful situation. He was full of the Spirit, free from all bitterness at his unjust sentence. He took that man and ministered to him and brought him into deep peace. He described his experience of the last night of the retreat in this way:

> How can I express in words the experience of Sunday evening? We gathered and prayed for the gift of the Holy Spirit in words and singing continuously. It was an experience of great joy. We prayed collectively for the gift of the Spirit for ourselves. Then we went individually to be prayed with. There was a continuous stream of people going up. Everyone was joyfully singing or praying. I could see great joy on the faces of everyone. It was out of this world.

As those prisoners, many of them deeply impressed by bad and bitter memories, opened their hearts to the Lord and forgave themselves, with the same forgiveness they received from the Lord, there was "great joy on the faces of everyone". Even the often grim circumstances of prison cannot rob people of the joy of the Lord.

The prisoners discovered the liberating power of forgiveness. First of all we had turned to the Lord for the forgiveness that we all need. Then I had invited them to forgive everyone who had ever hurt them, to share with them the forgiveness they had received. And finally I had asked them to forgive themselves. I asked them to say this prayer: "Lord, I thank you for forgiving me my many sins. Now, Lord, I forgive myself. I thank you for the wonder of myself. I thank you that I am precious in your sight."

Every morning we should begin the day with thanking God for the wonder of ourselves; every night, as we examine our conscience and ask pardon of God for the sins of the day, we should also forgive ourselves. That is the way of peace.

Healing of Memories

The experience of Christ's gift of abundant life can be impeded by sad and bitter memories. Memory is a great gift from God. Through memory we can recall all God's gifts. But if memory is abused it becomes a great burden. People can use their memory as a storehouse for resentment, anger and bitterness. As the Scottish poet Robbie Burns said, "they nurse their wrath to keep it warm".

To experience Christ's abundant life we must live on every word that comes from the mouth of God. This is true too of our memory. Scripture tells us how to remember:

> Bless the Lord, O my soul,
> and all that is within me,
> bless his holy name.
> Bless the Lord, O my soul,
> and do not forget all his benefits. (Ps 103.1-2)

The Holy Spirit directs us, in this passage, to bless God, not just with our thoughts and our prayers, but with "all that is within me".

What is "within me"? Everything that has ever happened in my whole life is within me. It is registered in that faculty we call memory. Each experience of life is logged in my internal, personal computer. I cannot consciously remember everything that has ever happened to me at the same time. I recall the different experiences of my life as I need to. I had hundreds of thousands of experiences last year. They are in my memory. But I am not thinking of them now. However, if I wish, I can go back to some event last February. I can recall how it happened and why, recall how I experienced it at the time; if it was a hurtful event I can feel again the pain it caused; if it was a joyful and affirming event I can relive the joy of that moment.

The hurtful and distressful events of life were bad enough when they happened. They robbed us of peace and joy for some time. If they become painful and resentful memories they can rob us of peace and joy for a lifetime. All those millions of past events have shaped us, action by action. An action from the past can float into our memory, charged with the intensity of resentment or bitterness, and seek to shape our response in the present. That is the power of memory.

The healing of memories is the only effective response to bad memories. Time does not really heal the memory. A person may live for many years without consciously recalling some sad or painful event of the past. Once, however, the painful memory surfaces the person may become sad or depressed or even very angry and resentful. I am sure you may have often been surprised to hear an old person suddenly pour forth bitterness about something which happened many years previously. The passage of time did not take away the bitterness; the memory registered the pain and the bitterness at the time and until that memory is healed the pain and the bitterness remain. In fact we simply talk about the person having painful or bitter memories.

God wants us to have grateful memories. Our memories should be patterned on the Holy Eucharist. The Eucharist, the Mass, is the grateful memory of the Church. When he gave us the Eucharist, Jesus said to us, "do this in memory of me". In all our eucharistic prayers we specifically remember:

> Father, calling to mind the death your Son endured for our salvation, his glorious resurrection and ascension into heaven, and ready to greet him when he comes again, we offer you in thanksgiving this holy and living sacrifice.

In the great eucharistic act of remembering we call to mind Christ's passion, death and resurrection and we give God praise and glory. We do not call to mind his cruel suffering in order to complain about it or to condemn his tormentors and executioners. We recall to praise God. In the same way we recall our own past sufferings, not to complain or condemn, but to give God glory: "Bless the Lord, all that is within me."

C.S. Lewis said "praise is inner health made audible". Past hurts, which fester in the memory as resentments, are healed through the simple prayer of praise: "Bless the Lord, all that is within me". As we act on this word of God, resentful memories become grateful memories. I refresh my memory not to complain but to give thanks.

The past is the past. I cannot change it. What I can change is the way I remember the past. I choose to remember resentfully or gratefully. If I remember resentfully the past continues to shape my response in the present. I will be in danger of acting out my resentments. If I meet the person against whom I carry resentments my "body language" will communicate them. He or she will be made aware that I am resentful and unforgiving. If I remember gratefully, the hurts of the past lose their power to influence my response in the present. I remember not to complain or condemn but to give God thanks. That is how the Christian spirit responds in each situation. St Patrick wrote, "Today, among heathen peoples, I praise and proclaim your name in all places, not only when things go well but also in times of distress. Whether I receive good or ill, I return thanks equally to God, who taught me always to trust him unreservedly."[13] I often think this is the origin of a very typical Irish response to tragedy, "Sure it could be worse, thank God": I have witnessed people of faith gain enormous strength in the face of some great suffering with those words.

Initially, of course, it may seem impossible to recall and give thanks. The pain may be too great. You must be patient with yourself. If, however, you cannot say "thanks be to God" as you recall some painful event, what are you saying? If you are not responding with a blessing you will be responding with a condemnation, even though you may not formulate it as such, and that painful event will remain unintegrated into your being and it will continue to have the power to make you sad or mad.

The grace of the healing of memories brings with it the awareness that I can become grateful for all the events of my past life and integrate them into the present. But I must make the decision. About some past event of my life I am free either to bless or curse. I cannot be saying to myself "I wish God would do it for me." God gives me the grace, but I must speak the blessing. I may have to go through all the stages of moaning and groaning, and protesting about what happened in the past, but if I want to be healed and live in the present I must let go of the past. The best way to "let go" is to place the past in God's hands and say "thanks be to God". In his loving providence God takes care even of the past. As Rowan Williams puts it so well, "if forgiveness is liberation, it is also a recovery of the past in hope, a return of memory, in which what is potentially threatening, destructive, despairing, in the past is transformed into the ground of hope".[14]

As I recall the sinful events of the past I ask God's forgiveness. Then I thank him that in and through the sinful events he was with me and took care of me. This is how the Church, in the great song of the Easter Vigil, thanks God even for the sin of Adam: "O happy fault, O necessary sin of Adam, which gained for us so great a Redeemer!" When we sincerely turn to God even our past sins are occasions for giving thanks.

As I recall the painful events of the past, the way I hurt myself or the way other people hurt me, I renew my forgiveness and then I thank God that even in and through these unjust and hurtful deeds he was with me. I seek to discern his presence, "walking the path of life with me", and together we thank God the Father.

I was once leading a parish congregation in this kind of healing prayer, emphasizing that no matter what happened, no matter how sinful or violent it may have been, Christ was present, suffering with the person, supporting and sustaining him or her. After the service a whole family came up to me. They were all crying. The mother spoke for them all. She said that twelve months previously her sixteen-year-old daughter had been murdered. Their greatest pain as a family was the thought of her being all alone and helpless as her assassin raped and murdered her. "Now", she said "we know she was not alone. Christ was with her." They were at peace in their grief.

That deep realization of Christ being with that young girl, as she was being brutalized and killed, came to her family because they were praying "We thank you, Lord, that even in the most distressing situation you are present". Until they introduced themselves, I did not know their tragic history at all. Had I known that they were in the church I would probably not have focused so much on thanking the Lord for his presence in all our distressing and sad situations. But they were obeying God's word and blessing God with all that was with them, with the pain and the agony of the memory of her death, and the gentle realization that Christ was with her dawned on them and brought them peace. That is the healing power of the word of God.

It is not the past event itself which changes, but the way we remember it. We begin to relate to the past in a new way. Recalling the past ceases to be the occasion for experiencing resentment and anger and becomes the occasion for glorifying God. As we recall and give thanks the wound in the memory is healed.

Jesus said: "they are happy who hear the word of God and keep it". The word of God to us about our memory is "all that is within me, bless his holy name". When we keep this word, when we live on it, when we really thank God with "all that is within", we experience the power of God's word through the healing of memories. "He sent out his word and healed them" (Ps 107.20).

I was once praying with a Presbyterian minister who had very bad memories of his childhood and, as a result, could not forgive or respect his mother. When he was nine years old, forty years ago, his mother divorced his father and married again. He had to live with his stepfather. The boys at school threw the divorce and second marriage up at him. They mocked him. He felt ashamed of his mother. He eventually became a minister in the Church of Scotland. Yet, despite the fact that he was preaching the Gospel, proclaiming the forgiving love of God, he could not bring himself to forgive his mother, much less honour her.

As we began to pray I asked him to close his eyes and imagine himself back at home in some familiar situation with his mother and stepfather. He got a clear picture of sitting at the kitchen table with them. Then I asked him to imagine Jesus coming into the kitchen. When he had a clear image of Jesus entering the kitchen I asked him simply to observe what Jesus did and to thank him. We prayed together for some time. I was thanking the Lord for his presence with the family and for his blessing on the family.

When we finished the prayer he was very moved. He told me that when Jesus entered the kitchen he had the clear impression of him sitting down at the table with them. The Lord then took his father's hand and his mother's hand and he placed his father's hand on top of his mother's hand. Then the Lord took his hand and placed it on top of both their hands and held it there. I asked him if that was how he married a couple and he said yes. He was, in imagination, officiating at the marriage of his parents!

While this symbolic gesture was happening in his imagination, I was thanking the Lord for his presence to and blessing on the family. The minister realized that all his life he had been condemning his mother for the second marriage; he was ashamed of her second marriage. Now as I began to thank the Lord for his presence in the family he was able to thank God for the second marriage. All the shame was gone. He received a great healing of memory. He said, "I am now going to get into my car and drive straight to see my mother." He had not seen her for a very long time!

As a footnote to this story it should be said that this minister was an expert counsellor. He was very well versed in the schools of modern psychology. He had come through extensive therapy himself. It was only, however, when he obeyed God's word and praised God with "all that is within" that he was delivered from deep shame and healed in his memory.

If there is something painful in your memory and if you really want to be healed, all you have to do is to humbly invite it, whatever it is, to bless God. Hold it patiently before God and say "thanks be to God". Once you begin to say "thanks be to God" over some painful event of the past, the process of the healing of memories has begun. Persevere with this prayer of gratitude, even when you feel you do not or cannot possibly mean it, and you will experience in time the healing of your whole memory.

True Self-esteem

Inner healing enables us to live gratefully in God's presence, accepting ourselves just as we are and thanking God "for the wonder of our being". As we "live by every word that comes from the mouth of God" we develop an unconditional, positive self-regard. We begin to see ourselves in the way God sees us. God sees us "as precious in his sight" (Isa 43:4) We begin to see ourselves in that light. We impose no more external "conditions of worth". Our true worth is within. Anselm Gruen writes:

> Our problem is that we are always looking for our selves outside: in confirmation by others, in instances of outward success, and in external security. But the self is to be found only within, in the inner world of our soul, in our true homeland. Bugental says that the country where we really belong lies within us, and there we are the undisputed rulers. If we do not rediscover this age-old truth, each in his or her own way, we are condemned to wander hither and thither, seeking consolation where it can never actually be found – in the outside world.[15]

True self-esteem flows from self-acceptance. Our formula is: Self-Knowledge + Self-Acceptance = Self-Esteem. Stanley Coopersmith, one of the earliest psychologists to study self-esteem, gave us this definition:

> By self-esteem we refer to the evaluation which the individual makes and customarily maintains with regard to

> himself: it expresses an attitude of approval or disapproval, and indicates the extent to which the individual believes himself to be capable, significant, successful and worthy. In short, self-esteem is a personal judgment of worthiness that is expressed in attitudes the individual holds toward himself. It is a subjective experience which the individual conveys to others by verbal reports and other expressive behaviors.[16]

The act of esteeming self, or its opposite, disesteeming self, is an act of self- evaluation. Like all evaluation, self-evaluation must be based on knowledge. What knowledge about ourselves do we have for making an accurate evaluation? Where do we get this knowledge or information? Can we trust the source of this knowledge? Can we be certain that this knowledge on which we base our self-evaluation is true knowledge of who we are as individuals? These are basic questions, which we have to address, because in the area of self-esteem our biggest problem is distorted knowledge. We don't always know ourselves at any great depth. Yet, on the basis of this ignorance of self we often base our self-evaluations. And, what is more alarming, on the basis of other people's ignorance of us we too often base our self-evaluation. We take other people's evaluations of ourselves and make them our own.

God knows us through and through. He alone can evaluate us. And on the basis of God's knowledge of us he says we are "precious in his sight", we are "a new creation" (2 Cor 5.17), we are "God's work of art" (Eph 2.10). If that is how God evaluates us, how do we evaluate ourselves? God's evaluation of us must be the basis of our own evaluation of ourselves. But we do not automatically evaluate ourselves in the light of God's word. The Jesuit psychiatrist James Gill writes:

> Sociologic research in the United States has found that people evaluate their personal worth, not so much by looking

at themselves as by measuring their success. This appears true whether the assessment is based on material rewards or spiritual accomplishments. Again different individuals gauge their degree of success according to different criteria, but each generally learns in early life, from his parents, teachers, and other models, to adopt one of four principal scales of accomplishment. These include significance, competence, virtue and power.[17]

Coopersmith had earlier analysed the ordinary sources of self-esteem in a similar way:

> The four sources of self-esteem, and the four criteria employed to define success, are the ability to influence and control others – which we shall term Power; the acceptance, attention, and affection of others – Significance; adherence to a moral code – Virtue; successful performance in meeting demands for achievement – Competence. We should note that it is possible for an individual to attain high self-esteem by notable attainment in any of these four areas. This might occur even where attainment in other areas was mediocre or even poor... On the other hand, it is possible for an individual to attain notable success in an area that he does not regard as important, such as competence, and thus conclude that he is unworthy because he has not succeeded by the criterion he most values, such as virtue. Thus a man who is extremely capable in performing his occupation may nonetheless conclude that he is not successful because he does not fulfill the precepts he considers to be of major importance.[18]

The feeling of self-esteem, because it is about ourselves, is a unique source of human well-being. No success in my external world can bring me peace and happiness if I am not at peace in myself and happy with myself. Wealth, prestige, success and honours are all empty if I don't have appropriate true self-esteem. As Sullivan says, "Self-esteem is the way in which I relate to myself and the way I feel about myself."[19] Self-esteem touches my inmost being. If I don't feel good about myself nobody or no external thing can make me feel good. Self-esteem is an inside job. I myself am responsible for my feeling of either high or low self-esteem. Nobody makes me feel bad about myself. However, while that remains true it is also true that the way I was treated as a child, the way I was either approved of or disapproved of, formed within me, at a very young age, an attitude to myself which, if unchanged, will result in either approval or disapproval, high self-esteem or low self-esteem. As Kaufman says:

> Because we learn to treat ourselves precisely the way we either experienced or observed significant others to do, we learn to shame ourselves, hold ourselves in contempt, blame ourselves, hate ourselves, terrorize ourselves, and even to disown a part of ourselves that had been rejected and consistently enough cast away by a parent, whether intentionally or inadvertently. Such internal actions as these can additionally be mediated through the parent's internal representative, the identification image, which serves as the watchdog of the inner life, the gatekeeper of the unconscious... Hence we learn to speak to ourselves, to say the very things subvocally to ourselves which our parents originally said to us.[20]

Our self-esteem, then, is very involved with the way in which our parents saw us and how they treated us and how they spoke to us. We begin to have the same attitudes to ourselves that they had; we begin to say the same things to ourselves that they did; and we begin to have the same high or low expectations of ourselves that they had. It is as if we made a tape recording of our parents' voice and now we can play it over and over again, if we wish.

A helpful distinction has been made between *foundational self-esteem* and *secondary self- esteem*. Foundational self-esteem is what the child receives through good enough parenting. The term "good enough parenting" says to parents that they don't have to be perfect. If they love and accept the child and cherish it for its own sake they are being "good enough parents". When the child feels accepted for its own sake and not just for being "a good child", when it feels it can trust its parents totally, when it is free to be itself and not simply the fulfilment of its parents' dream, then its true self will emerge. This acceptance is the foundation of all future development in the child. As Carrol Saussy writes:

> Most people who work as counselors would probably agree that the most essential ingredient in adult self esteem, the foundation of adult self esteem, is the experience of having been genuinely accepted and cherished as a child. Genuine acceptance leaves the infant free to discover her or his true self.[21]

The child will now develop what Saussy calls "good enough foundational self-esteem". The opposite of this self-esteem is a weak foundational self-esteem. Saussy writes:

> When a child becomes alienated from her own genuine feelings because a parent has signalled that such feelings are unacceptable, and the child has been inundated by the parent's mirrored expectations of how she or he must behave, the child will struggle to conform to a false self and that can at best result in false-self esteem. "I will be loved because I will be the good child they want me to be."[22]

Secondary self-esteem builds on foundational self-esteem.

However, when there is little foundational self esteem and there is instead an "as-if personality", a defensive secondary self esteem can be built on the sham foundation of the false as-if self. Thus secondary self-esteem can be either authentic or counterfeit. When secondary self esteem represents an adaptation to the demands of the false self, it is defensive and counterfeit.[23]

But good secondary self-esteem can be built up by the adult.

Secondary self esteem achieved through good relationships and reworking of early ideology can be remedial. That is, weak foundational self-esteem can be shored up when an adult is helped through authentic, respectful relationships to recover her lost child or true self. Recovery means validating authentic feelings, sensations, and needs. The result of such confirmation can be good enough true-self esteem.[24]

This means that a person whose foundational self-esteem has been impaired, because of some problem in early development, can recover from that original set-back and develop a healthy sense of self and a good self-esteem. In other words, healing of the causes of poor self-esteem is possible. And we have discussed the key to this healing in some detail namely "living in the house of the creative word", forming our self-image on God's word, and living "by every word that comes from the mouth of God".

True and False Self

We speak of the "true self" and the "false self". Saussy identified the origin of the false self when she said that the child says to itself: "I will be loved because I will be the good child they want me to be." In such a situation the child will conform to all the wishes of the parents and it will begin to develop a false self. If the child continues to develop in this way, seeking to be loved by meeting the expectations of others, it will lose touch with its true self and the false self will begin to dominate. As the child develops it will posit its personal worth outside itself. Its worth will be found in "being the good child" or in pleasing others. A false self is being formed.

Charles Whitfield in his book *Healing the Child Within*, uses a variety of terms interchangeably to speak about the true self. He writes "I use the following terms interchangeably: Real Self, True Self, Child Within, Inner Child, Divine Child and the Higher Self."[25] As a psychotherapist Whitfield is seeking to focus the mind on that part of ourselves which is most authentic, the healthy self, or the self which expresses itself when we are most ourselves, most genuine, most creative.

The human person is a complex being in which the authentic and unauthentic coexist, the true self and the false self live side by side. A person's genuine happiness and fulfilment depend on which "self" predominates.. We recognize that there is a part of the total being which we call "self" that is genuine, authentic and real – the true or real me; and there is a part which is not genuine, which is unauthentic and false, the false self or the codependent self. Psychologists can tell us how this unauthentic self, or false or codependent self, was formed. When we live to meet other people's expectations, when we feel that we must conform and please others if we are to be loved and accepted, then we present a false self; we develop a mask, a persona, an "as-if personality" and we present this false self to others. This false self will be the way we feel others want it to be: pleasing, ingratiating, assertive or submissive. It is not our real self that is expressing itself, rather it is the false self trying to be what we think others expect it to be.

The true self, in the words of Heather Ward, is "my capacity for God".[26] In her view the essence of our selfhood resides in our capacity for continuing acceptance of the gift of God's life-giving Spirit. Our openness to God, our receptiveness and responsiveness to God constitute the heart of the self. Self, then, is not a thing, an object, like any member of the body; self is dynamic openness, an ability to receive from and to respond to God. Ward points out that self, as "our capacity for God", is prior to all the qualities of the self. The qualities of the self are expressed through the personality, but the personality is not synonymous with self. The personality expresses something of the self but it cannot express the whole self. We cannot reduce self to personality. One person may have a "wonderful personality", another person may not. But in both there is a true self, equal in dignity and worth. Thomas Merton wrote: "For me to be a saint means to be myself. Therefore the problem of sanctity and salvation is in fact the problem of finding out who I am and discovering my true self."[27] A constant theme of Pope John Paul II is that it is only in Christ that we can "find ourselves".

Merton, in his many spiritual writings, popularized the distinction of the true and false self. He used a great variety of terms to express the true self: "true self", "inner and hidden self", "creative and mysterious self", "inner self" "inmost self", "real self", "deepest and most hidden self". This rich variety of terms shows that Merton was not engaging in a rigorous, scientific analysis of the true self but rather that he was exploring in a literary, poetic, imaginative way. He makes us aware of our "deeper selves". Beneath the surface, beneath all that we do or say or feel, there is something else, something that gives coherence and unity to my very being. That something, created by God, is the gift of my true self. It cannot be measured; it cannot be known directly; since it is the image of God it can only be known by knowing God. This self, this secret, hidden source of my unity and coherence, transcends all individual expressions of it, while at the same time it permeates each one. It is my capacity for God. In each situation I have the capacity to receive God's Spirit and respond to God. That is my true self. This capacity for God is a gift of God's creative and redeeming love and as such cannot be fully comprehended or defined by psychology. This spiritual capacity for God is not the same thing as psychological self-realization. On the psychological level the false self can easily come to realization, whereas on the spiritual level the false self can never become a capacity for God. As Thomas Del Prete writes:

> Merton establishes firmly that the true self is in no sense a psychological self-realization...Whereas self-realization for the false self would entail fulfillment of its psychological need for self-affirmation and will to self-assertion, "true" self-realization entails inner discovery of the "someone that one already (potentially) is, the person one is truly meant to be", that is, "the very self who finds". The inner, spiritual nature of the true self precludes psychological definition or explanation.[28]

We would have to say that the true self, understood as our capacity for God, our openness to God and our ability to respond to God, is an object of our faith. It is created by God, not by ourselves. And, while a person may develop a strong personality he or she cannot develop his or her true self. He or she can only discover it and live in harmony with it. Since the true self is God's creation, our capacity for God, true self-esteem is an appropriate response to God's gift. True self-esteem is simple gratitude to God for the gift of self. Living a spirituality of true self-esteem brings us to the source of the self we esteem, namely to God. In esteeming ourselves as God's people we are honouring God.

Notes

[1] Veritatis Splendor, 19.

[2] Constitution on Divine Revelation, 10.

[3] Veritatis Splendor, 85.

[4] Constitution on the Church in the Modern World, 22.

[5] The Redeemer of Man, 10.

[6] Ibid., 30.

[7] Constitution on the Church in the Modern World, 91.

[8] In 1973 I was asked by my Provincial to establish a centre for renewal in our stately mansion, Hawkstone Hall, which had been for many years our seminary. Priests and religious sisters and brothers come from all over the world to our renewal courses. Each year there are three residential renewal courses. Each course lasts three months. Sixty-five participants are accepted on each course. Since their inception these courses have been the source of great spiritual and personal renewal for thousands of religious men and women and priests. It was into this atmosphere of prayer and renewal that the priest in question walked.

[9] Cited in Leanne Payne, Restoring the Christian Soul through Healing Prayer, Eastbourne: Kingsway, 1992, p. 31.

[10] The Redeemer of Man, 10.

[11] Constitution on the Church, 4.

[12] C.S. Lewis, Fern-Seed and Elephants, Glasgow: Fontana, 1975, p. 40.

[13] Confessions of St Patrick, 36.

[14] Cited in L. Gregory Jones, Embodying Forgiveness, Grand Rapids MI: Eerdmans,1995, p. 177.

[15] Anselm Gruen, The Spirit of Self-Esteem, London: Burns & Oates, 2000, p. 30.

[16] Stanley Coopersmith, The Antecedents of Self-Esteem, San Francisco: Freeman, 1967, p. 5.

[17] James Gill, Human Development, no. 3, 1980, p. 34.

[18] Coopersmith, The Antecedents of Self-Esteem p. 38.

[19] James Sullivan, Journey to Freedom, New York: Paulist Press, 1987, p. 55.

[20] Gershen Kaufman, Shame: The Power of Caring, Rochester, Vermont: Schenkman Books,, 1991, p. 102.

[21] Carroll Saussy, God Images and Self Esteem, Louisville: Westminster/John Knox Press, 1991, p. 78.

[22] Ibid., p. 79.

[23] Ibid., p. 78.

[24] Ibid., p. 81.

[25] Charles L. Whitfield, Healing the Child Within, Deerfield Beach, FL: Health Communications, 1987, p. 9.

[26] Heather Ward, The Gift of Self, London: Darton, Longman & Todd, 1990, p. 125.

[27] Thomas Merton, Seeds of Contemplation, New York: New Directions, 1949, p. 26.

[28] Thomas Del Prete, Thomas Merton and the Education of the Whole Person, Birmingham, AL: Religious Education Press, 1990, p. 113.

5

Barriers to Inner Healing

St Paul reminded the Thessalonians that the Gospel is "still a living power among you who believe it" (1 Thess 2.13). In another well-known passage we read, "the word of God is living and active" (Heb 4.12). When we are dealing, then, with the word of God we must always realize that through this word the power of God becomes present and active. As Jesus himself says, "the words that I have spoken to you are spirit and life" (Jn 6.63).

The inner healing ministry shows us that as we take the word of God seriously, as we begin to live on it and keep it in our heart, we experience its healing and liberating power. In the last chapter we considered three different areas of inner healing, namely the healing of the self-image, the healing of relationships and the healing of memories. In each area the healing comes through hearing the word of God and acting on it.

Ministering, then, through the word of God we have the power to bring people into a new experience of the healing love of God. As we teach people to listen to the word, to welcome it and respond to it, we see them grow in the Spirit and rejoice in God's healing love. Normally those who sincerely seek inner healing receive it.

If a person is sincerely seeking inner healing, but is not receiving peace, we have to discern what is blocking the peace. There are five major barriers which we will look at: lack of self-acceptance, unrepentance, unforgiveness, guilt, and finally bondage, which we will look at in the next chapter.

Lack of Self-acceptance

We have seen that "self-acceptance is the root of all things". It is the root cause of our being at ease with ourselves. Self-rejection, on the other hand, is the root cause of lack of ease, dis-ease, with self. If the person is in the destructive process of rejecting self, inner healing will be blocked.

When the person is not receiving Christ's gift of peace we have to begin a discernment process to investigate whether the cause for the lack of inner healing is a root of self-rejection. We have to keep clearly in mind the counselling principle that the presenting problem is never the real problem. A very good priest once came to me with a big problem. Two of his confrères in community completely ignored him. They would not greet him or acknowledge him. Being a sensitive man he felt very hurt. He also felt worried because he wanted to show them love and forgiveness. He was anxious that, since they were persisting in their coldness towards him, his forgiveness and love might also turn cold. He was convinced that these two men were the big problem in his life. He prayed daily that the Lord would change their hearts. He had others pray with him for the same intention. Still he was worried.

His two confrères were the presenting problem. They were not the real problem. The cause of the real problem was not in them; it was in himself. We had to identify that cause. As he talked about his relationship with them it became clear that, despite his experience of their rejection, he had a daily expectation that one morning they would be glad to see him! In normal human relationships that would be a realistic expectation. But his whole experience of these two men should have told him that it was quite unrealistic for him to expect them to become friendly towards him. In fact, such an expectation was not only unrealistic, it was also laying a great burden on them.

They could not meet his expectation. As a consequence the priest felt rejected and hurt. The prayer that he was receiving for the hurt did not bring peace because the object of the prayer was to get rid of the rejection and not to get rid of his unrealistic expectation. The presenting problem was the rejection; the real problem was his daily, unrealistic expectation that two enemies would become his friends. Once he saw that the cause of the hurt which he was experiencing was not the rejection, but the expectation that the rejection would not happen, he was able to take power over his own life again. He began to see that at the heart of his problem there was a self-rejection. His self-acceptance was conditional. It depended on his being accepted by others, especially by these two men who were, for their own reasons, unfriendly towards him. By his unrealistic expectation he had given these two men tremendous power over his life. The first step in the healing process was not to ask God to change them, but to ask for the grace to withdraw the expectation, to give up the non-verbal demand that they should become friendly towards him.

I shared with him the story of a religious sister who had a similar problem in her community. She had made a directed retreat with me and was experiencing great peace. There was a sister in her community whom she feared. She said that this sister would disturb her whole peace again in a matter of days! I gave her these simple steps for prayer:

1. Each day thank God for the wonder of herself, then thank God for the wonder of her sister;

2. Thank God for all the good things he is doing in her life, then thank God for all the good things he is doing in her sister's life;

3. Make allowance for all her own failures, as she asked God for pardon, and then make allowance for all her sister's failures.

She told me later that shortly after her return from the retreat this sister said to her one morning, "You have become very nice to me all of a sudden"!

There is a great lesson in this for all of us. The sister on retreat sincerely felt that this other sister was cold and unfriendly. As a result, her "body language" communicated her fear and apprehension in her presence. She was living in the house of the destructive word in regard to this sister. Then she began to live in the house of the creative word of God, she began to thank God for the sister and acknowledge all the good things God was doing in her. The "body language" changed and instead of communicating fear and apprehension she began to communicate acceptance and appreciation.

Again, we see that the presenting problem was not the real problem. The presenting problem was the other sister's apparent coldness; the real problem was that she herself, sensing coldness, was non-verbally communicating her fear and apprehension. God healed this relationship not by changing the other sister but by changing herself. She was unconsciously rejecting herself. She was unhappy, defensive and apprehensive because her self-acceptance depended on the approval of the other sister. When that was not forthcoming she lost her peace.

If people have lost heart, if they are feeling that the problems of life are too many and too heavy, it is most necessary to help them, in the words of Pope John Paul II, "to find themselves". The pain, the failures, the sins, the frustrations of life initiate the process of self-rejection. This process is reversed when the person draws near to Christ. As John Paul says,

> They must with all their unrest, uncertainty and even their weakness and sinfulness, with their life and death, draw near to Christ. They must, so to speak, enter into him with their own self, they must "appropriate" and assimilate the

whole reality of the Incarnation and the Redemption in order to find themselves.[1]

The very things which cause self-rejection – namely, sinfulness, weakness and failure – become the graced opportunity of self-discovery when we bring them all into Christ.

Unrepentance

Sin alienates us from God, from others and from self. The only way to overcome this alienation is through repentance. Sometimes we try to make ourselves believe that we have really repented. As Jeremiah said, "The heart is devious above all else" (Jer 17.9). If I have sinned and remain unrepentant I will not experience the peace of Christ which comes through inner healing.

In the Introduction to the new Rite of Penance we have this description of *metanoia* or repentance:

> We can only approach the Kingdom of Christ by *metanoia*. This is a profound change of the whole person by which we begin to consider, judge, and arrange our life according to the holiness and love of God, made manifest in his Son in the last days and given to us in abundance. The genuineness of the penance depends on this heartfelt contrition. For conversion should affect the whole person from within toward a progressively deeper enlightenment and an ever-closer likeness to Christ.[2]

Metanoia, or conversion, implies "a profound change of the whole person". As Bishop Morris Maddocks says, it is "a reorientation of the whole personality".[3]

Remorse for sinful behaviour may lead to repentance but it is not in itself repentance. Remorse is the pain of the conscience passing judgement on the sinful action; repentance enables the person "to begin to consider, judge and arrange life according to the holiness of God". True repentance is a rebirth. By his forgiving grace God touches the depth of our conscience where the wound of sin cries out for healing. As the sinner turns to God with all his or her heart, God's powerful action of forgiveness grants the person wholeness and integrity again.

A Presbyterian lady came to me for healing prayer on one occasion. She had cancer. Before we began to pray she said to me, "I know that I must now cleanse my heart from all sin, I must confess all my sins to God and receive his pardon". She made a very moving and complete confession to the Lord. "Now," she said "I am ready to receive healing prayer."

Unconfessed sin will always block the peace of Christ. We cannot simultaneously seek peace from the Lord and at the same time hold on to the very thing which has robbed us of peace. A lady once rang me and asked me to pray for the healing of memories for a man with whom she had sexual relations. They had a bad disagreement and he did not want to see her again. It turned out that she was a married woman! When I said to her that the only healing for adultery was repentance and confession she became most irate.

The good news, of course, is that God delights in forgiving our sin and taking away our guilt. Unconfessed sin will always cause inner distress and block the flow of peace. This is how Scripture graphically describes the conflict:

> While I kept silence, my body wasted away
> through my groaning all day long.
> For day and night your hand was heavy upon me;
> my strength was dried up as
> by the heat of summer.

> Then I acknowledged my sin to you,
> and I did not hide my iniquity;
> I said, "I will confess my transgressions to the Lord,"
> and you forgave the guilt of my sin. (Ps 32.3-5)

God meets our confession and repentance with the gift of total forgiveness. Clinging to unrepented or unconfessed sin blocks the experience of God's healing love.

When inner healing is being blocked through lack of repentance the person should always be encouraged to bring his or her sin confidently to the Lord in the sacrament of confession or according to his or her own denominational practice. Sometimes, sadly, the sin remains unconfessed because the person has had a very bad experience of confession. If that is the case one should pray for the healing of that bad memory before encouraging the person to confess. The person should be asked truly to forgive the confessor and to put his or her trust again in the sacraments of Christ.

Unforgiveness

Unforgiveness is a major block to inner healing. Just as openness to God, in love and contrition, is the prerequisite for the grace of repentance, so openness to one's neighbour, in acceptance and acknowledgement, is the prerequisite of the grace of forgiveness. If a person seeking the healing of relationships continues to experience resentment and bitterness the block may be an unforgiving heart.

Forgiveness brings with it a total acceptance of the other person. We no longer see the person with the eyes of the sinned against; rather, we see the person with the eyes of a sinner who has also been forgiven. Accepting means that we do not try to forget the wrong. Rather, as we let go of resentment or bitterness we begin to remember in a new way.

Gordon Wilson of Enniskillen gave the whole world a perfect example of Christian forgiveness. He was standing with his daughter at the Remembrance Day parade in Enniskillen in 1987 when a massive IRA bomb exploded without warning and killed eleven people. Among the dead was his daughter Marie. He spoke on prime-time television (I saw him on CNN news in San Francisco) about the great loss he and his wife had sustained. Then he thrilled millions around the world by saying that he and his wife had forgiven the bombers and that they prayed each night for them. The world would have understood if Mr Wilson had proclaimed his undying hatred for the bombers. Some, indeed, were disappointed that he did not do so. But this devout Methodist knew his Lord and he knew that Our Lord, who forgave his own executioners, gives to each of us that same power to forgive. There are no half-measures in Christian forgiveness. There are no unforgivable people in a Christian's world.

The blockage in inner healing may be a half-hearted assent towards forgiveness. I once had a frustrating experience trying to help a very hurt woman. Each time she would go through the motions of forgiveness. I thought she had forgiven. But the resentments came back. Then I began to realize that instead of really forgiving she was simply trying to find good excuses. When she found what she thought was a good excuse she would forgive. The next day, however, the excuse did not seem all that good and her resentments returned. In the end I had to recognize that she was not prepared to offer true Christian forgiveness in the sense in which C.S. Lewis describes it:

> Real forgiveness means looking steadily at the sin, the sin that is left over without any excuse, after all allowances have been made, and seeing it in all its horror, dirt, meanness and malice, and nevertheless being wholly reconciled to the man who has done it. That and only that is forgiveness.[4]

Before any inner healing could bind up her wound this woman had to pray for the grace of fundamental conversion.

The person who has been deeply distressed by hurts and unforgiveness can only enter into peace by welcoming the gift of *metanoia*, of that radical conversion which brings with it a "reorientation of the personality". Faced with the impasse of unforgiveness in the heart of a hurt person we should encourage the person to listen to the words of Jesus, "Father, forgive them, for they don't know what they are doing", and we should ask him or her to pray for that same grace. We should encourage the person with the assurance that he or she must be patient and ask for the gift of the Holy Spirit. In Chapter 9 we will look at the process of forgiveness in detail.

Guilt

When we do wrong we experience "guilt feelings". The reason for these feelings is that we recognize that we have acted in a way which is contrary to our sense of what is right and good. If we had no reason, no conscience, we would never experience "guilt feelings". The frightening thing about the psychopath is that he or she can commit terrible evil, like murder, without ever feeling guilty.

Feeling guilty, then, is the appropriate way to feel when we sin. In sinning we violate not just some moral law but also our own conscience, our own sanctuary. The Second Vatican Council tells us that "conscience is people's most secret core, and their sanctuary. There they are alone with God whose voice echoes in their depths."[5] It is in our conscience that we become aware of God's law. The Council said:

> Deep within their consciences men and women discover a law which they have not laid upon themselves and which

they must obey. Its voice, ever calling them to love and to do what is good and to avoid evil, tells them inwardly at the right moment: do this, shun that. For they have in their hearts a law inscribed by God. Their dignity rests in observing this law, and by it they will be judged.[6]

When we act against our conscience we feel guilty. That is the sign of a healthy conscience. Indeed, it is the grace and light of the Holy Spirit inviting us to turn again to God and seek forgiveness.

When we acknowledge and confess our sin and ask God's pardon, God takes away our sin. Normally too we are freed from all feelings of guilt and know instead the renewed peace of the Lord. While feelings of guilt and shame are the direct consequence of sinful behaviour, feelings of peace and joy are the direct consequence of having our sins forgiven. Once our sins have been forgiven, feelings of guilt would no longer be appropriate. Such feelings, instead of calling us to conversion, would be enticing us to doubt or even deny the forgiveness which we have received.

We can speak, then, of good guilt and bad guilt. Good guilt is the appropriate response to sin; bad guilt is the inappropriate response to forgiveness. The appropriate response to forgiveness is praise and thanksgiving. "Go in peace, your sins are forgiven." The inability to give praise and thanks may be a sign of bad guilt.

Bad guilt blocks inner healing. The person continues to feel guilty even though God has forgiven his or her sins. The bad guilt must be addressed in prayer. I find the most effective prayer for dealing with bad guilt is the Eucharist. In the Second Eucharistic Prayer we pray, after the Consecration, "We thank you for counting us worthy to stand in your presence and serve you." I ask the person to hear these words deeply, and every time he or she comes into God's presence to let that be the first prayer. Every time he or she is attacked with the bad guilt the immediate response should be, "I thank you for the wonder of myself", and "I thank you that you count me worthy to stand in your presence and serve you."

Locked into bad guilt we often find a sense of shame. The person is ashamed not of some bad action in the past but of himself or herself. He or she may be a shamed person. Our society uses shame to control people. The mother may say to the little child, "Don't do that, shame on you"; the teacher may say to the young boy, "Your older brother would never do that, shame on you"; an irate parent may say to the adult son or daughter, "You ought to be ashamed of yourself." Bad guilt, compounded by shame, presents a formidable obstacle to inner healing. With such a person we have to start with the basics, namely the healing of the self-image. We have to teach the person to live by the creative word of God, which assures the person that he or she is "precious in God's sight". The person must not live by the destructive word, which accuses him or her of being an object of shame.

We should introduce the person suffering from this bad guilt to St Bernard's approach:

> What I can't obtain by myself, I appropriate to myself with confidence from the pierced side of the Lord because he is full of mercy. The mercy of God, therefore, is my merit. And what about my righteousness? O Lord, I shall remember only your righteousness. It is also mine because you are God's righteousness for me.

If none of the four barriers mentioned in this chapter is present, or if all barriers have been resolved, and yet the person is not receiving peace through inner healing prayer, we may then have to consider the presence of the fifth barrier. This is a bondage of some kind, and will be explored in Chapter 6.

Notes

[1] The Redeemer of Man, 10.

[2] Rite of Penance, 6.

[3] M. Maddocks, The Christian Healing Ministry, London: SPCK, 1985, p. 12.

[4] C.S. Lewis, Fern-Seed and Elephants, Glasgow: Fontana, 1975, p. 41.

[5] Constitution on the Church in the Modern World, 16.

[6] Ibid.

6

Breaking the Bondage

In praying for inner healing we have the word of God to guide us and the Spirit of God to empower our ministry. The word of God has been called "a light for my path and a lamp for my way". With that light we can enlighten the inner world of the person. We have seen how the light of the words "I thank you for the wonder of myself" lights up the whole dimension of self-acceptance. So, too, the words "bless the Lord, O my soul, and all that is within me bless his holy name" light up everything that is going on in the memory bank. And the words "forgive seventy times seven" enlighten the quality of relationships with those who have hurt us. We need this light in the ministry of inner healing.

It sometimes happens that someone, despite getting the "all clear" in the areas of the four barriers discussed in the last chapter, is still not receiving the gift of peace. Then we have to discern, with the help of God, what is blocking the peace. If the person is open to the Spirit of God in his or her own spirit – open to accepting self gratefully, open in repentance and forgiveness – but is still not receiving peace, we have to discern whether there is some form of evil spirit, some demonic interference, with the person's freedom.

In the Introduction to the new Rite of Penance we are told that "discernment of spirits is indeed a deep knowledge of God's working in the human heart, a gift of the Spirit, and an effect of charity" (no. 10). We believe that there are three spirits at work in the life of each human being, namely God's Spirit, the human spirit, and the evil spirit. We have to discern what comes from each of these spirits.

The Holy Spirit is the spirit of love, joy and peace; the spirit of truth and freedom; the spirit of counsel and fortitude; the spirit of encouragement and consolation. We discern his presence through his fruits. The evil spirit is the spirit of darkness and fear; it is "the father of lies" and "a murderer from the beginning"; it is the "unclean spirit", the "accuser of the brethren" and the enemy of our human race. We can discern the evil spirit's presence also through its destructive fruits.

Sometimes the barrier to inner healing may be the action of the evil spirit. This does not necessarily imply that the person who is the victim of the evil spirit's action is bad or evil. It may mean simply that while the person was very hurt or weak the evil spirit took advantage and used the hurt or weakness to form a bondage.

The story of two mothers, both suffering from the shock of murder in their families, will illustrate this. While I was on a parish mission in the west of Scotland a lady came to see me during a house Mass. Everyone at the Mass was coming to confession. She came in and said, "I can't go to confession, but I would like to talk." I presumed that she could not come to confession because she may have been married outside the Church. "Oh no", she said, "I can't forgive, so there is no point in me going to confession."

She then told me her sad story. Her only son was serving a life sentence for the murder of a young man. She was convinced that this young man and his family goaded her son beyond endurance and that he had no intention of killing. But he was found guilty and sentenced. Now her heart was full of hatred. "I have no peace", she said, "because I hate them and I can't forgive them." I asked her if she would like to forgive and she responded immediately, "I would love to. It is like a cold stone in my heart."

She was a good woman, a devout Catholic. I saw her at all the services of the mission. I had not realized until then she was not coming to the sacraments. Here was a very clear case of a woman deeply desiring to do the Christ-like thing and forgive and not being able to do it. Through the tragic killing on her son's part she now found herself bonded through hatred with the family whose son he killed. She was in real bondage. She was not free.

I explained to her that Jesus would set her free and give her the power to forgive. As I was praying with her I bound that evil spirit of hatred in the name of Jesus and silently commanded it to depart and never return. I then asked the Lord to fill her with his forgiving love. The hatred and coldness in her heart immediately left her and she knew she had forgiven them. During that house Mass she received Holy Communion for the first time in years with great joy.

Almost exactly the same situation confronted me some months later in the east of Scotland. I was conducting a renewal day in a parish. A lady came to see me and with her beautiful sad voice she said, "I have just come in for a chat because I can't go to confession." Again I thought she may have been married outside the Church. "No", she said, "my son was murdered in London and since then I can't come to the sacraments because I hate his murderer and his mother. If I can't forgive there is no point in me going to the sacraments, is there?" When I asked her whether she would like to be able to forgive I got the very same answer. "I would love to. It's like a cold stone in my heart."

I explained to her that Jesus would take away the stone and enable her to forgive. "I hope to God he will", she said, "because I am demented." I used exactly the same silent prayer, binding the evil spirit in Jesus' name and commanding it to depart. I asked the Lord to fill her with the Holy Spirit and with his forgiving love. She was instantly set free. Later on that day she came up during the healing service for the anointing. She was full of joy and said, "I have forgiven him and I have forgiven his mother and I am praying for them."

She was a good woman but through the murder of her son she was bonded in hatred to the man who killed him and also to his mother. She had lost her freedom in relation to them. She was in bondage to them. This bondage robbed her of the very means of peace. She could not forgive. In both this and the former case the bondage had to be broken before the women came into the freedom of forgiveness.

I use this image to help myself think about what is actually happening in these cases. Suppose you are washing the dishes in the sink and you cut your finger on a broken glass. You immediately rinse the finger under the tap, put on some TCP and a plaster. Your finger will be fine in the morning. But suppose you cut your finger on a rusty nail and carry on doing what you are doing all day. By evening there is a throb in the finger and then you wash it and put a plaster on. How will the finger be in the morning? It will have festered. Before the finger heals you have to get the poison out. For the healing of the nice, clean cut all you need is the TCP and the plaster; for the healing of the festered finger you have to get the poison out first.

Sometimes, I think, a similar thing happens in the spiritual world. If a person has been hurt badly, but the wound remains clean and uninfected, inner healing is all that is needed. But if the evil spirit infects the wound with its poison of bondage, inner healing will not work. First the bondage must be broken.

We call this ministry of breaking the bondage "the deliverance ministry". The deliverance ministry is based on a number of truths which not all Christians accept. As I mentioned in Chapter 1 there are some theologians and Scripture scholars who simply deny both the reality of evil spirits and the consequent need for any ministry of deliverance. As I wrote, "Biblical theories have pastoral implications. Demythologizing the New Testament teaching on the reality of evil spirits declares the ministry of exorcism, in all its forms, obsolete. The discernment of the need for exorcism belongs to pastors and ministers rather than to academics and theologians." Had I approached my ministry to the two women mentioned above with the conviction that there are no evil spirits and consequently there can never be a need for deliverance, they would have remained in the bondage of hatred and unforgiveness. I would have tried to comfort, console and counsel them. But they had received all that from their parish community. And still they were bound in hatred.

I understand why many priests and ministers today never use this ministry. For the first ten years of my ministry I never saw any need for it. When people came with problems I would listen to them, counsel them to the best of my ability, hear their confession if they wished to confess and send them off with a word of encouragement. I remained very much on the level of counselling. I celebrated the sacraments of anointing and reconciliation for sick and hurting people. Outside the sacramental context, however, I had no prayer ministry for them. I never prayed with them for inner healing. When I was going through the seminary I never heard of a ministry of inner healing. Similarly, I never saw the need for deliverance because I had forgotten altogether about the reality of evil spirits. I looked exclusively for psychological explanations; outside the sacramental celebrations I applied only counselling skills.

On 24 September 1975, during the first three-month renewal course at Hawkstone Hall, where I was director, I went to confession to a visiting priest, Fr Wilfrid Brieven, who was, at the time, secretary to Cardinal Suenens. Fr Brieven not only heard my confession but he prayed over me for a very long time. A deep peace settled on me and I knew that I was making a completely new commitment of my life to Christ. I also knew that my whole approach to priestly ministry would have to change. I was experiencing help in an altogether new way, not through the counselling skills of an expert but through the faith of a priest.

Describing the effects of this spiritual event in my own life I wrote three years later:

> The way Fr Brieven prayed with me in celebrating the sacrament of reconciliation became the norm of my own celebration. And I saw marvellous results. As I prayed with people for inner healing I saw them being freed from deep resentments and anger, from bitterness and jealousy, from all kinds of things which had been robbing them of joy in the Lord. In the sacrament of reconciliation I saw the difference between the simple absolution with a few words of encouragement and the extended prayer for inner healing.[1]

I found my whole ministry of listening and counselling transformed through a prayer ministry for inner healing. On many occasions the prayer did not work. That always puzzled me. Why does a prayer for inner healing, which brings such peace to one person, fail to bring the same peace to another, even though the other seems to have exactly the same hurt and the same desire to be freed? I gradually became aware of the barriers to inner healing which I discussed in the last chapter. But I also became aware that besides barriers of a psychological or moral nature there could be barriers of a demonic nature. I had recovered my faith in the Church's teaching on the reality of evil spirits. I became aware that in some cases where the people failed to receive inner healing the real barrier was in some mysterious way outside themselves.

My first experience of the deliverance ministry was while I was trying to help a young married woman. She was married to a long-distance lorry driver. He had to drive all over Europe, sometimes as far as Rome. He would be away from home for days on end. She had become very suspicious that every time he went abroad he was being unfaithful to her. When she came to see me she was almost demented with these suspicions. She explained that he was a good, loving and kind husband and that he would feel awful if he ever knew that she had such suspicions. At the same time she could not get them out of her mind. As I prayed with her I became aware that this suspicion was an evil thing, attacking her peace and threatening to undermine and destroy her marriage. I found myself saying, "I bind this suspicion in the name of Jesus Christ and I command you evil spirit leave this daughter of God the Father and never return." The prayer was said in silence. Then I prayed aloud for the Lord to bless her marriage and to fill her home with his Holy Spirit. She experienced a great peace and complete release from the suspicion. She began to send all her married women friends to see me. They came with the same request, "I believe you have a great blessing for married couples." She had told them about her release from her terrible suspicion and how God had blessed her marriage. She taught me how to speak about the ministry of deliverance. It is a great blessing.

As I reflected on that pastoral experience it became obvious to me that I would have wasted my time if I had tried to bring her to peace simply by counselling. She knew that the suspicion was irrational. She could give me all the good reasons why her husband would not be unfaithful. Yet she was, in her own words, "demented". I was deeply impressed myself at what had happened. Nothing in my theological formation had trained me to do what I had just done. I realized that I had performed some form of exorcism or deliverance and that some kind of evil spirit had departed. I had taught moral and pastoral theology to students for the priesthood for six years and I had never even mentioned a ministry of deliverance or exorcism. Looking back on those years I have to say that although I never formally gave up belief in the Church's teaching on evil spirits, my faith was totally inactive. I was aware that possession by the devil could take place in rare cases; I was also aware that if that happened the bishop would appoint a holy, wise and ascetical priest to deal with it. It would be no concern of mine.

I realized that throughout the Catholic Church, in most, if not in all the seminaries where priests were being trained, there would be no teaching on this ministry. That is why I said that I understand why so many priests and ministers do not use this ministry. Like myself, nobody taught them about it. The more I became aware of the need for this ministry, however, and the more I saw suffering people being set free, the more concerned I became to locate this ministry within my own Catholic tradition. It was an Anglican priest, Christopher Neil-Smith, who taught me how to do this. In 1977 Christopher, the official exorcist for the diocese of London, conducted a workshop on exorcism for a group of Catholics at Hawkstone Hall. He has a most blessed ministry of deliverance and has helped hundreds of people into freedom in the Lord. He began by saying that he was delighted and surprised to be addressing a group of Catholic priests, religious and laity on the subject of exorcism because he had learned most of what he knew from Catholic sources. This remark forced me to go back to the sources. I went back to the Church's tradition, to the manuals of moral theology which had been used in Catholic seminaries for centuries, and, to my great delight and relief, I discovered that what Christopher Neil-Smith said was true. Confessors throughout the centuries had been encouraged to use a silent prayer of simple exorcism to set people free.[2]

The new Anglican Report, *A Time To Heal*, has a very helpful chapter on "Deliverance from Evil". The authors review the state of the ministry of deliverance and exorcism in the Church of England and emphasize the need to work collaboratively with the medical world.

> The decision to perform a service of exorcism should only be taken after other avenues have been explored and the

risks assessed. An exorcism should only be carried out by a priest or other minister who has the authority of the bishop to do so. Counselling should form an important part of the process, and pastors should ensure that they are supervised and that they work closely with the medical and other professionals. Where a person is already receiving other professional care, it is desirable to work collaboratively in a multidisciplinary approach, respecting one another's professional boundaries. There should be provision for pastoral care and counselling following the service. In each diocese people should be carefully chosen and authorized for this ministry and we recommend that they have access to consult and work with other clergy and medical colleagues.[3]

The Anglican Report, among other recommendations, says: "we endorse the normal practice of suitable people having episcopal authorization for deliverance ministry and the widespread appointment of diocesan teams". The Report also says: "clergy and lay people involved in this ministry should have appropriate training and supervision".[4] If the Anglican Church acts on this Report we should see a very mature ministry of deliverance develop. In many places in the Catholic Church the deliverance ministry is being developed. The fact that Pope John Paul II had performed three exorcisms since he became pope made headlines in the papers. The official exorcist in Rome frequently speaks about the need for this ministry. But we don't have any real pastoral discussion on the need for deliverance in the Catholic Church, nor do we have an official, mature reflection on the nature of the deliverance ministry such as is found in the Anglican Report. We need such a reflection.

The Prayer for Deliverance

The prayer for deliverance is not an appeal to Jesus to drive away the evil spirit. It is a command, in the name of Jesus, directed to the evil spirit. This command is normally given in silence. The fact that, as a result of this silent command, a troubled person is set free is a clear sign that an intelligent being heard the command and obeyed.

Once we become aware that there is need for deliverance we should focus all our attention on the Lord. We do not focus on the evil spirit. The following steps can be helpful:

1. A prayer of praise. Devote a little time to rejoicing in Christ's great victory over Satan and evil;

2. Pray for Christ's protection on everyone involved. Christ is present to defend us and therefore we should have no fear of the evil one. We pray, "Lord, we claim your victory now. You are our protector and our deliverer";

3. A prayer of binding. Before we command the evil spirit to depart we bind it in the name of Jesus. For instance, "I bind in the name of Jesus Christ every evil spirit". If we have discerned that there is a spirit of fear or a spirit of unforgiveness it would be appropriate to say "I bind you, spirit of fear, or spirit of unforgiveness, in the name of Jesus Christ";

4. The direct command to the evil spirit to depart: "I command you in the name of Jesus Christ, unclean spirit, to depart from this beloved son or daughter of the heavenly Father and never return. I command you to go to Jesus." We let the Lord himself send the evil spirit to where it belongs. It is important to keep praising the Lord while commanding the evil spirit to depart. For instance, if there is a spirit of fear present you could be

praising the Lord audibly and silently commanding the evil spirit to depart. When the person begins to join in the praise of God that is a good indication that something is happening and that the spirit has left. If the person cannot join in the praise he or she is still bound in some way. At that stage it is often helpful to ask the person what is going on inside and how he or she is feeling. We keep praising until the person feels free to join in;

5. Invoke the Holy Spirit to come and fill the person afresh. Where there was darkness we pray for the Spirit of light; where there was fear we pray for the Spirit of courage; where there was sin we pray for the Spirit of holiness. Since the person has been chosen to be "the temple of the Holy Spirit" we should invoke the Spirit with great confidence. The Spirit comes to reclaim, sanctify and fortify what rightly belongs to him.

We should never tell the person that we are going to pray for deliverance. It is sufficient to say, "Let us bring this problem, this inner wound, this bondage to the Lord and ask for his blessing." We silently command the evil spirit to depart. I believe the principal reason for this way of proceeding is this: we can never be a hundred per cent certain that we are dealing with an evil spirit. If there is no evil spirit present the deliverance is not necessary. But, if the person has been told that he or she needs a deliverance, and then nothing happens, he or she would be left feeling that the evil spirit was still there. That is why we must always follow the prudential rule of silent prayer and refrain from indicating, in any way, that an evil spirit is at work in the person.

Sometimes it will be very important to have a follow-up ministry to the person. We should direct them to a good faith-sharing group or prayer group where possible and encourage the person to become actively involved in his or her local Christian community. The lack of a warm, welcoming community, where people know how to pray with one another, and know how to build one another up in the faith, is an incalculable impoverishment of Christian ministry today. With so many men and women, all endowed with the Holy Spirit, many of whom are already gifted and experienced in this ministry in the Spirit, there is no excuse for people to have to go without the appropriate Christian ministry.

Notes

[1] *Anointed with the Spirit,* London: NSC Publication, 1978, p. 50.

[2] St Alphonsus Liguori speaks for the Catholic tradition when he writes: "Private exorcism is permissible to all Christians; solemn exorcism is permissible only to ministers who are appointed to it, and then only with the express permission of the bishop" *(Theologia Moralis,* III, 2, 492).

   The basic distinction is between simple and solemn exorcism. According to Noldin, the Jesuit manualist, simple exorcism is for the purpose of curbing the devil's power, while solemn exorcism is for the purpose of driving the devil out. Those who are possessed by the devil need solemn exorcism. This exorcism is reserved to the bishop. Noldin, however, encouraged confessors to use simple exorcism more frequently: "It is much to be desired that ministers of the Church should perform simple exorcism more frequently, remembering the words of the Lord: In my name they shall cast out demons – this exorcism can be performed without the knowledge of the person" *(Theologia Moralis,* III, 59).

   Prummer, a Dominican manualist, said: "Experience teaches that sometimes in the confessional, exorcism can be used secretly, without the penitent's knowledge" *(Theologia Moralis,* II, 365). In the same volume Prummer also wrote: "Nowhere is it forbidden to the laity to use private exorcism." Marc, a Redemptorist manualist, wrote: "Private exorcism is lawful to all, especially priests, nor is there any special permission of the bishop required" *(Institutiones Morales Alphonsiane,* I, 622).

   The new Code of Canon Law states: "No one may lawfully exorcise the possessed without the special permission of the local Ordinary. This permission is to be granted by the local Ordinary only to a priest who is endowed with piety, knowledge, prudence and integrity of life" (Canon 1172). When a person is obviously possessed the bishop must be approached. He must be part of the discernment. For a more detailed discussion of this point see the book by Cardinal Suenens, *Renewal and the Powers of Darkness,* London: Darton, Longman & Todd, 1983.

[3] A Time To Heal, London: Church House Publishing, 2000, p. 180.

[4] Ibid., p. 181.

7

Inner Healing and the
Sacraments of Reconciliation
and Eucharist

Catholics automatically think of the barriers to inner healing in the context of the sacraments: they would see forgiveness, repentance, freeing from guilt as the specific grace of the sacrament of reconciliation.

On Easter Sunday evening the risen Lord said to his disciples, "Receive the Holy Spirit. If you forgive the sins of any, they are forgiven them; if you retain the sins of any, they are retained" (Jn 20.22-23). The Church's faith crystallized into the firm belief that the Easter gift of the risen Lord, namely the power to forgive sins through the Holy Spirit, remains with the Church. It remains specifically in the sacrament of reconciliation. When someone asked the great G.K. Chesterton why he became a Catholic, he said simply, "because I wanted someone to use the power Jesus gave to the Church and say to me your sins are forgiven". The desire to hear the forgiveness of God proclaimed through the power of the Holy Spirit is one of the deepest desires of the sinful heart.

Throughout the history of the Catholic Church there has been a great emphasis on confession and the forgiveness of sin. The practice of "going to confession" was one of the distinctive hallmarks of Catholics. The experience of the Church throughout the centuries has been that a good confession brings great peace to the soul. Fr Bernard Häring describes peace:

> The biblical concept of peace is amazingly comprehensive. It includes salvation, wholeness, integrity, healthy and healing interpersonal relationships, cultural, economic and social relationships and transformations which serve the cause of peace and of wholeness and integrity.[1]

God's gift of peace is lost through serious sin. If we knowingly and willingly do what is contrary to God's will our soul is bereft of peace. Only God's gift of forgiveness, received through our contrite confession, restores our peace. While the peace of soul is lost through serious sin, our peace can be disturbed by what the new Rite of Penance calls "the wound of sin".

Wound of Sin

In the Introduction to the New Rite of Penance we read: "Just as the wounds of sin are varied and multiple in the life of individuals and of the community, so too the healing which penance provides is varied" (no. 7).

We recognize two effects of sin: sin as an offence against God, causing an alienation between God and self; and the wound of sin, that is the inner hurt caused in a person by the sinful action or words. The sin itself will be manifested in a cold, deliberate, malicious act of one kind or another; the wound of sin will reveal itself through some kind of reaction. Just as a person in pain may cry out, so a person with the wound of sin may very well "strike out".

For the sin itself we need God's forgiveness; for the wound of sin we need the Lord's healing. Both are signified in the words of absolution: "Through the ministry of the Church may God give you pardon and peace". Pardon is for the sin; peace is for the wound of sin.

New Emphasis

This is a new emphasis in our understanding of the sacrament of reconciliation. We always saw the sacrament as the great means of forgiveness. We did not, however, always focus on the healing power of the sacrament. We had lost sight of what the new Rite of Penance calls "the wound of sin".

If a husband and wife, for instance, have a nasty row, and they do not take time to show each other loving forgiveness, the hurts which they have inflicted on one another will remain unhealed. Very little provocation will be needed to spark off the next row. If they continue in this cycle of fighting, without really healing the wounds through loving and tender forgiveness, they will reach a stage in their relationship where the slightest thing will provoke a row. They will not be able to communicate with each other; they will blame one another; they will no longer be able to trust one another. The breakdown in their relationship will be caused by the inner wounds which they have inflicted on each other and which have been allowed to fester. They may even be blaming each other for the lack of communication or trust, whereas the real cause will be the unhealed wounds.

If they bring their wounds to the sacrament of reconciliation they will experience healing. They will be able peacefully to face the task of rebuilding their relationship. While the wounds remain unhealed this task will be impossible for them. Even if only one of them seeks healing for the wound of sin the total relationship will be transformed. The healed partner will no longer be re-acting out the inner wound, but responding in love.

Barbara tells the story of how God healed her marriage. She was praying for God to do something about her husband. He had no faith and was reacting negatively to her strong faith. As she was asking God to change him for the better God let her see that he was not pleased with her prayer. She was sitting in judgement on her husband. The Lord taught her to pray this prayer: "Lord, heal my marriage, but begin with me."

She kept praying this prayer faithfully. She began to notice that her husband was going out on the same evening each week. He never said where he was going. On his return one evening he took her completely by surprise and announced that he was about to be received into the Church. His mysterious weekly trips were for instruction in the faith. From the moment she began to take responsibility for their relationship and ask God to begin the healing of their marriage in her, their relationship improved. The whole relationship changed because she was willing to ask the Lord to heal the wounds in herself.

The sacrament of reconciliation is for the healing of all inner wounds. When a Catholic speaks to me about a painful or broken relationship I always suggest that we should bring the relationship to the celebration of the sacrament and seek reconciliation. In the celebration we listen to the word of God; we pray for discernment; we enter into deeper sorrow for sin; we confess our sins; we receive God's forgiveness for our sins and healing for the wounds of sins; in our purpose of amendment we promise God to do our best to avoid these sins and the occasion of sin in the future.

As the person seeks reconciliation with God in the sacrament he or she can be led to seek reconciliation with the person who has caused hurt and offence. The confessor leads the person in forgiveness prayer.

Role of Confessor
The New Rite of Reconciliation describes the confessor's role in this way:

> By receiving repentant sinners and leading them to the light of the truth, the confessor fulfils a paternal function: he reveals the heart of the Father and shows the image of Christ the Good Shepherd. He should keep in mind that he has been entrusted with the ministry of Christ, who mercifully accomplished the saving work of human redemption and by mercy and by his power is present in the sacrament (no. 10).

The penitent should experience, in the way in which the confessor receives him or her, "the heart of the Father". The confessor's role is to mirror the love and compassion of God. The penitent may arrive broken-hearted, feeling cut off from God and full of confusion, shame and distress. In the confessor, the penitent should meet understanding, total acceptance, and great encouragement. The confessor has to reflect to the penitent the very acceptance of God the Father and the forgiving love of Christ.

The specific gift of confession is this: people can bring to the sacrament all sins, no matter how serious, for which they are sorry; they can confess them with the certainty that God forgives the sins and heals the wounds of sin; and they have the assurance that confidentiality is guaranteed. In the strictest sense people can come to the sacrament and unburden themselves.

One lady who shed her burden described what happened in this way:

> It isn't easy to confess sins of a sexual nature, and it isn't easy to break a long established habit. I had a strong habit of masturbation which bothered me for many years. You prayed over me and I felt a great weight being lifted off me and a tremendous feeling of joy welling up within me. I knew I had been set free. What I could not achieve by my own efforts and good resolutions over the years had

happened instantaneously by the power of the Holy Spirit made effective through your prayer. I will celebrate for ever the joy of that moment.

God's answer to sinfulness is forgiveness, healing and liberation. Too often the human response is one of rationalization. We pyschologize away the sin. This lady had a strong, compulsive habit. Some would say to her, "Don't worry, this can't be sinful. You haven't the freedom to commit sin." Such an approach takes the whole problem out of the Lord's hands and leaves the penitent a victim to his or her compulsion.

Instead of trying to rationalize away the sin we encourage the penitent to be open to the presence of the Holy Spirit for the full forgiveness of sin. As we say in the words of absolution, "God the Father of mercies, through the death and resurrection of Jesus Christ, you have reconciled the whole world to yourself and you have sent the Holy Spirit among us for the forgiveness of sins". The heart of the sacrament is this new, forgiving, sanctifying and healing presence of the Holy Spirit; Christ's Easter gift of the Spirit is for the forgiveness of our sins. It is also our divine physician's remedy for the wounds of sin. The sacrament, celebrated with contrition for sin, truly "binds up the broken heart".

The Eucharist and Inner Healing

We celebrate the Eucharist "for the glory of God". St Irenaeus told us that the "glory of God is the human person fully alive". This means that when God is being glorified something is happening in us. We are being changed. Everything in us which is in any way opposed to being fully alive in the Spirit is being dealt with. If it is a sin, it is being forgiven; if it is a wound of sin, it is being healed; if it is a bondage of sin or evil, we are being set free.

The Second Vatican Council reminded us that the Eucharist is the very centre of our worship of God and our life as a people of God:

> The other sacraments, and indeed all ecclesiastical ministries and works of the apostolate, are bound up with the Eucharist and are directed towards it. For in the most blessed Eucharist is contained the entire spiritual wealth of the church, namely Christ himself our Pasch and our living bread, who gives life to people through his flesh – that flesh which is given life and gives life by the Holy Spirit. Thus people are invited and led to offer themselves, their works and all creation in union with Christ. For this reason the Eucharist appears as the source and summit of all preaching of the Gospel.[2]

In the celebration of the Mass we have "the entire spiritual wealth of the church". Everything that Christ has done for us is present in the mystery of the Mass. As the Council says:

> At the last supper, on the night he was betrayed, our Saviour instituted the eucharistic sacrifice of his body and blood. This he did in order to perpetuate the sacrifice of the cross throughout the ages until He should come again, and so to entrust to his beloved spouse, the church, a memorial of his death and resurrection: a sacrament of love, a sign of unity, a bond of charity, "a paschal banquet in which Christ is received, the mind is filled with grace, and a pledge of future glory is given to us".[3]

We participate in the mystery of the Eucharist by engaging in four very familiar activities: we listen, we respond, we offer, we receive.

We listen. We listen to the life-giving word of God in the first part of the Mass, the part we call "the liturgy of the Word". We should listen with that hunger of Jeremiah: "When your words came I devoured them" (Jer 15.16). The Mass is a privileged moment for hearing the Word of God.

People sometimes complain that the Mass is boring. After years of trying to think how to make the Mass "more interesting", it dawned on me that for many people the Mass is boring because they do not listen to the word of God. The person who does not listen to the proclamation of the word of God during the "liturgy of the Word" will never be able to enter into the mystery of the Mass.

The Second Vatican Council reminded us that in the Eucharist the Church lays before us two tables, the table of the word of God and the table of the body of the Lord. We must feast at both tables. Listening avidly to the word of God opens our mind and heart to the healing which the Eucharist offers us. "Say but the word and I shall be healed".

We respond. Hearing the word of God enables us to respond to what God is saying to us. We have multiple responses in the Mass: prayers for mercy and forgiveness; hymns and prayers of praise and thanksgiving; prayers of intercession and petition; times for silent adoration and contemplation.

In the first part of the Mass we deal with a major barrier to inner healing, namely unrepentance. We acknowledge that we are sinners. We ask God's pardon. Putting our heart into the responses deepens our faith and spiritually prepares us for the sacrifice which we offer to God. As St Paul said, "I appeal to you therefore, brothers and sisters, by the mercies of God, to present your bodies as a living sacrifice, holy and acceptable to God, which is your spiritual worship" (Rom 12.1).

We offer. The offering that we make of ourselves to God is symbolized in the gifts we bring to the altar. We bring gifts of bread and wine. These gifts represent ourselves, represent "all that is within us". We offer to God not just what is good and healthy, but what is sinful, weak and wounded. In the Mass we should consciously offer to God all our weaknesses: all our inner wounds and pain; all resentment, anger and bitterness; all our broken promises and sinful failures. Our gifts of bread and wine represent all that.

A new relationship is created between the one who offers the gift and the one who receives it. The one who offers is the *giver* the one who receives becomes the thanksgiver. When you give a gift to a friend your gift represents yourself; it represents your love for your friend. By receiving your gift your friend reciprocates your love. He or she says, "Yes, I am your friend and I am grateful to you for your gift of friendship."

The same dynamic is at work when we give gifts to God. Our gift represents our love. God becomes *thanksgiver* to us for the gift we offer to him in the Mass. In God's grateful acceptance of the offering we are making of ourselves we have the answer to the first great barrier to inner healing, namely lack of self-acceptance. God's total acceptance of us in the Mass should become the norm of our self-acceptance. God accepts all those things about us which we may find it hard to accept: our sinfulness and weakness, our frustrations and disappointments. Everything within us, which could cause self-rejection, should be offered to God in the celebration of the Eucharist.

During our celebration of the Eucharist we have the most appropriate moment to act on Pope John Paul II's insight: "They must with all their unrest, uncertainty and even their weakness and sinfulness, with their life and death, draw near to Christ. They must, so to speak, enter into him with their own self, they must 'appropriate' and assimilate the whole reality of the Incarnation and the Redemption."[4]

In the Eucharist we have the complete reality of the incarnation and redemption present sacramentally on the altar. As we offer ourselves to God we open our whole lives to be filled with "all the fullness of God" (Eph 3.19).

We receive. Having offered our gifts, the symbol of ourselves, the priest prays, "Let your Spirit come upon these gifts so that they may become for us the body and blood of Jesus Christ your Son." The bread and wine, which represent us before God, through this wonderful action of the Holy Spirit, become for us the body and blood of the Lord. Our gifts have been accepted and transformed by God. We too have been accepted. There is, therefore, no place in our life for any false guilt. We can pray with confidence: "We thank you for counting us worthy to stand in your presence and serve you." The Mass deals with all bad guilt. Because God counts us worthy, we accept ourselves as worthy.

During Mass, too, we are invited to dismantle that other barrier to inner healing, namely unforgiveness. After the Consecration we invoke the Holy Spirit for the gift of unity: "May all of us who share in the body and blood of Christ be brought together in unity by the Holy Spirit." We surrender everything which is opposed to this unity in the Spirit: unforgiveness, condemnation and rash judgements; envy and jealousy; all lack of love.

In a symbolic gesture we manifest our unity. The priest says, "Let us offer each other a sign of peace." At this stage we generally offer our hand in peace and friendship to those around us. The sign of peace is extended not just to those who are physically close to us in the church. It is for those who are emotionally close to us, even though they may be many miles away. In the Eucharist we are in the right space to offer our full forgiveness to everyone in our life.

Having shared that sign of unity we are now ready to receive. We receive Holy Communion. Our very approach to the altar is a proclamation that we are at peace with our brothers and sisters. Holy Communion is not just an act of union between Christ and the individual; it is a declaration of our intention to live in unity with all. Holy Communion is a sacrament. As the Council put it: it is "a sacrament of love, a sign of unity, a bond of charity".[5] Holy Communion presupposes that I love and forgive my enemies; it assumes that I have confessed all grave sin and that I am sorry for all my sins; it implies that I am actively seeking unity and peace with everyone in my life.

The bread of life which we receive in Holy Communion is rich in the Lord's promise: "I am the living bread that came down from heaven. Whoever eats of this bread will live for ever; and the bread that I will give for the life of the world is my flesh" (Jn 6.51). The "living bread" which we receive in Holy Communion is for the life of the world. It is for that abundant life which the Lord came to give to each of us. Consequently, as we celebrate the Eucharist, as we feast on the "living bread" of Christ's body, we can say with great confidence, "say but the word and I shall be healed".

Entering into the mystery of the Eucharist, "appropriating and assimilating" Christ's redeeming work of salvation in the Eucharist, is the sacramental way of inner healing. We often, however, need help to do so. All the other forms of inner healing ministry should have as their aim the joyful participation in the Eucharist where God is glorified as we become, in St Irenaeus' words, "fully alive".

Notes

[1] For further reflections on these sacraments see my book *The Healing Power of the Sacraments,* Redemptorist Publications, 1984

[2] Decree on the Ministry and Life of Priests, 5.

[3] Constitution on the Sacred Liturgy, 47.

[4] The Redeemer of Man, 10.

[5] Constitution on the Sacred Liturgy, 47.

8

Praying for Physical Healing

Prayer for physical healing is much more straightforward than praying for inner healing. We see a person who is obviously sick, or in pain. We impose hands on the person and ask the Lord to heal. We can pray like that anywhere, at any time. "But I don't have a gift of healing" some people may say. That may be true, but they do have a gift of prayer. We are talking not about healing so much as about *praying*. The ministry is not "a healing ministry", it is a "ministry of prayer for healing". The ministry is not what we do through our own gifts, but what we do "in the name of Jesus". Jesus himself said, "In my name... they will lay their hands on the sick, and they will recover" (Mk 16.18).

Sacrament of Anointing

We have, of course, an official prayer for healing in the Church. St James wrote: "Are any among you sick? They should call for the elders of the church and have them pray over them, anointing them with oil in the name of the Lord. The prayer of faith will save the sick, and the Lord will raise them up; and anyone who has committed any sins will be forgiven" (Jas 5.14-15). In the Catholic Church we recognize this anointing in the name of the Lord as "the sacrament of the sick".

A sacrament is a personal encounter with the risen Lord. We believe that Jesus meets the sick person in love and forgiveness and with the gift of "life in abundance". The Second Vatican Council tells us that, in this sacrament, priests "by the anointing of the sick... console those who are ill".[1] Through the vagaries of our history the sacrament of the sick became the "last anointing", extreme unction. The sacrament was not administered to the sick person until he or she was in danger of death. While the sick person was still fighting for life, the sacrament was not celebrated. As a result, we have no tradition in the Church of preparing the sick for their anointing. In the not-so-distant past, indeed, it would have been almost impossible to sit down with a sick person and start preparing for the celebration of the anointing. That would have been perceived as a preparation for death. The relatives would have objected.

We have a very different perception of the purpose of the sacrament today. In the Rite of Anointing we read:

> This sacrament gives the grace of the Holy Spirit to those who are sick: by this grace the whole person is helped and saved, sustained by trust in God, and strengthened against the temptations of the Evil One and anxiety over death. Thus the sick person is able not only to bear suffering bravely, but also to fight against it. A return to physical health may follow the reception of this sacrament if it will be beneficial to the sick person's salvation. If necessary, the sacrament also provides the sick person with forgiveness and the completion of Christian penance (no. 6).

The purpose of the sacrament is to "give the grace of the Holy Spirit to those who receive it"; it is "to relieve the sick"; it is for healing and wholeness, both spiritual and physical. The Church in celebrating the sacrament today prays very directly for the healing of mind and body. The expectation in our hearts, as we celebrate the sacrament of anointing, must correspond to the prayers on our lips.

A religious sister once rang me and asked if she could bring a lady, Pamela, who was suffering from Multiple Sclerosis, for anointing and prayer. They would have to make a journey of over three hundred miles. I almost panicked. What if nothing happens? The poor woman, after such an effort and such a long journey, would be very disappointed! I realized that I was looking for an excuse to say no. Instead, thank God, I said yes.

I met this lady again, fourteen years after her visit. She told me that the Lord had completely healed her of MS. She kindly agreed to share her testimony with the readers of this book. She wrote to me on 3 March 1994 as follows:

> I was first diagnosed as having MS (Multiple Sclerosis) in April 1975. That followed years of doubt and worry that perhaps there was nothing really wrong with me after all: despite a lot of trouble in walking and a lack of sensation in my legs. For a long time the doctors thought I was suffering from spinal disc problems – and, indeed, I had two operations for disc trouble, one in 1969 and the next in 1974. It was after the last one that it was realised that something else was amiss. By then I was also having "bladder problems" which finally led to total incontinence. It was only then that I was tested for MS and the diagnosis confirmed.
>
> During the years 1975–1978 I gradually became more disabled. I could only walk a short distance before pain would bring me to a halt; the lack of co-ordination in my legs spread to my hands, so I devised a way of teaching which required virtually no writing on the blackboard but used "ready prepared" OHP transparencies; and the loss of feeling in my legs meant that I needed hand controls to drive a car. In the summer of 1978 I had a Urinary Diversion operation in order to cope with the bladder incontinence.

I think it was in January 1979 that my head called me to her office one day. She asked me if I would be prepared to drive her to Hawkstone Hall one day towards the end of February… When she went on to explain to me that the reason for the trip was so that Fr Jim McManus could pray with me to be healed, I found myself in a quandary. For the next few weeks I wondered, "Help! How do I get out of this?" A surprising reaction I suppose, but it made me take a good look at myself. I found I was scared to be healed because I was unsure of my identity without MS. I had gone beyond accepting the disease as God's will for me to using it for my very identity. It had become a crutch on which I depended so much that I didn't know who I would be without it. I suppose I lived for the acclaim people gave me for carrying on stoically; I used the disease to avoid doing what I did not really like doing. I had shut God out and not only accepted MS, but allowed it to become my god so that my life was an "ego trip" instead of a "God trip". Now the question was posed: "was I prepared to let go of myself and let God in – even if that meant giving up the identity I had built up for myself?"

Finally the day for the trip arrived. We left Glasgow early one morning and drove to Hawkstone Hall, in my hand-controlled car, in time for lunch. After lunch, Jim led us to a small room. I cannot remember very much about the surroundings – my mind was still in turmoil. Although I knew I wanted whatever God wanted, I was still somewhat apprehensive. All I remember clearly is Jim saying he would use the prayers of the Anointing of the Sick and anoint me. And that is simply what he did.

We were very soon on our way back to Glasgow. Immediately I felt a deep sense of peace; gone was the turmoil that had been with me since the visit was suggested. I experienced a feeling of tremendous energy and happiness that lasted for weeks. I also vividly remember the surprise at not feeling tired the next day from such a journey. But it was the following Sunday that I was to experience the full meaning of healing. I was in the bath in the early evening and, for the first time in at least three years, I felt the water. Just to make sure, I turned on the hot tap again and felt the warmth of the water lap around my legs. You can imagine how I felt! I was singing and shouting for sheer joy. I wanted to share it with my friends, but there was no one at the other end of the telephone line! It was a precious moment God and I had together – and one I shall never forget. But the most important change that took place was the fact that I knew God loved me for who I was, not for anything I could do for him – but just because I was me.

It took me a year to persuade the doctors that I didn't need to waste time on hospital visits any more and a little longer to persuade the DHSS that I didn't require a Mobility Allowance and the DVLC that I could use my feet to drive normally.

Ten years later my Urologist had to reverse the diversion (as a result of a kidney problem which I had developed in the past two years). He was convinced that I would be incontinent again, and offered me counselling to help come to terms with that condition. Imagine his surprise when he realised that I was fully continent; as he remarked, even if it was simply a case of misdiagnosis, my bladder should not work after lying unused for ten years. He maintains that there is no doubt that there has been a "Divine intervention"; as he put it, "there is definitely no medical explanation".

Pamela's testimony is full of enlightening observations. She had to struggle with the question Jesus asked the paralysed man at the Pool of Bethzatha: "Do you want to be made well?" (Jn 5.6). In that struggle she realized that she had come to depend on her sickness. It was her crutch. Not only that, it was becoming the source of her identity, even her god. Pamela's reflections on her feelings bring out well the difference between disease and illness. While disease affects the body, illness affects the way the sick person copes. Pamela's illness meant that she was beginning to cope by depending on the MS, as "her crutch". Her friends admired her courage. She kept on being a very successful teacher. And she could use her sickness to avoid what she did not want to do.

While Pamela was trying to find a way out of coming for anointing and healing prayer, I was momentarily trying to find a way of stopping her from coming. The journey would be too much: if she didn't get a healing, after such a long and exhausting journey, she would be bitterly disappointed. Pamela describes the moment of ministry in this way: "All I remember clearly is Jim saying he would use the prayers of the Anointing of the Sick and anoint me. And that is simply what he did." She makes it very clear that the healing came through the sacrament of anointing. Within the Rite of Anointing we have both the ministry of the word and the ministry of the anointing with prayer for healing. Let us remind ourselves of the various moments in the celebration:

1. The priest welcomes those who gather for the anointing and says, "My dear friends, we are gathered here in the name of the Lord Jesus Christ who is present among us." This gives the celebration its focus: Christ is present;

2. Having called everyone present to a deeper faith awareness of the presence of Christ, the priest then says, "Let us therefore commend our sick brother/sister to the grace and power of Christ, that he may save him/her and

raise him/her up".

Right at the beginning of our celebration, then, we commit the sick person to the power of Christ. In the case of Pamela, her friend and I would have very consciously and confidently placed her in Christ's hands;

3. We are then invited to prepare ourselves for "this holy anointing" by acknowledging our own   sinfulness and our need for God's gracious forgiveness. (The sick person has the opportunity to celebrate the sacrament of reconciliation at this moment also);

4. The Word of God is then proclaimed from the Gospel or one of the other New Testament writings. This proclamation calls the sick person and those present to a renewed faith in the healing love and power of Christ;

5. The priest preaches a short homily or shares his faith in the sacrament after the proclamation of the word. I normally simply remind the sick what the Church believes about this sacrament. In the Introduction to the new Rite of Anointing we read: "This sacrament gives the grace of the Holy Spirit to those who are sick: by this grace the whole person is helped and saved, sustained by trust in God, and strengthened against the temptations of the Evil One and anxiety over death." I would have pointed out to Pamela that she was about to receive from God a new gift of the Holy Spirit and I would have invited her to open her whole heart to welcome this gift;

6. Then all present begin to pray for the sick person. This time of prayer is concluded with the words "Give life and health to our brother/sister on whom we lay our hands in your name." The priest lays his hands on the sick person's head and invites the family, or close friends, or other parish ministers to do likewise;

7. The priest anoints the person. He can either use the oil that was blessed by the bishop at the Chrism Mass in Holy Week or he can bless the oil himself. This prayer of blessing builds up the sick person's faith for the anointing: "God of all consolation, you chose and sent your Son to heal the world. Graciously listen to our prayer of faith: send the power of your Holy Spirit, the Consoler, into this precious oil, this soothing ointment, this rich gift, this fruit of the earth. Bless this oil† and sanctify it for our use. Make this oil a remedy for all who are anointed with it; heal them in body, in soul, and in spirit, and deliver them from every affliction. We ask this through Our Lord Jesus Christ." A powerful prayer of blessing in which the Church concentrates the mind and heart of all present on God's healing love;

8. After this preparation through the asking of pardon for sin, the renewal of faith through listening to the word of God, and the prayers of the community the sick person is then anointed with the words, "Through this holy anointing may the Lord in his mercy and love help you with the grace of the Holy Spirit. May the Lord who frees you from sin save you and raise you up";

9. The priest leads those present in more prayer for healing. One of the prayers set out in the rite reads as follows: "Lord Jesus Christ, our Redeemer, by the grace of your Holy Spirit cure the weakness of your servant… Heal his/her sickness and forgive his/her sins; expel all afflictions of mind and body; mercifully restore her/him to full health, and enable him/her to resume his/her former duties, for you are Lord for ever and ever."

The liturgical rite of the sacrament prepares the person for real openness to the Holy Spirit. All the elements of openness are there:

the confession of our sins; the listening to the word of God; the renewal of our faith in God's healing love; our willingness to receive a new gift of the Spirit. Whoever celebrates the sacrament with this openness always receives a great blessing. It may not always be the blessing of physical healing, but it will certainly be a blessing of inner healing. Pamela first became aware of her inner healing: "I felt a deep sense of peace: gone was the turmoil that had been with me since the visit was first suggested." And she identified inner healing as the greatest gift which she received: "But the most important change that took place was the fact that I knew God loved me for who I was, not for anything I could do for him – but just because I was me."

Not everyone, as we know, experiences physical healing through the anointing as Pamela did. A priest who reviewed my book *The Healing Power of the Sacraments* made the comment that I only mentioned the "successes". What about all the times when people did not experience healing? I presume he meant physical healing and I cannot answer this question. We do the asking. God does the healing. I would love to see every sick person healed. But God loves them infinitely more than I do. And God is with them in the sacrament.

When we are celebrating the sacrament of anointing we believe that Christ himself is present, blessing the sick person through our ministry and filling them afresh with the Holy Spirit. We ask Christ with total confidence to heal the sick person in body, mind and spirit. Then we leave the final result to him. We cannot say that in Pamela's case the sacrament was a success but in John's case, because he did not receive physical healing, it was a failure.

Jane, a paralysed woman, was preparing to go to Lourdes with great faith. She was convinced that she would be healed. A confrère of mine, who was her close friend, feared that she would return very disappointed. On her return she was still paralysed. My confrère said to her, "Were you very disappointed when you weren't cured?" "Oh, no", she said, "I received something much better. I received the grace to accept myself just as I am. So, I am very happy."

Healing means wholeness and wholeness is the effect of spiritual well-being, not just physical well-being. If, for instance, a selfish, arrogant, mean man goes into hospital with a cancerous tumour and comes out a selfish, arrogant and mean man, without a cancerous tumour, the cancer was cured, but the person was not healed. On the other hand, if he came out of hospital a loving, kind, generous man, in a terminal condition, he would have been healed although the cancer was not cured. Healing is what happens in the whole person, not just in the diseased organ. Jane was healed at Lourdes, healed through the grace of self-acceptance.

Pamela's story has deepened within me the conviction that we must give time to the celebration of the sacrament of anointing. We must have a lively faith in its healing purpose; we must involve as many of the family and friends as possible in the celebration, urging them to pray with faith; we must expect both inner and physical healing through the sacrament; we must ensure through preaching, teaching and witnessing, that the parish community is fully aware of the great healing gift God has given to the Church in this sacrament; the parish community must support the celebration of this sacrament just as it supports the celebration of the other sacraments.

How wonderful it would be if members of the parish visited the sick person in preparation for the anointing. They could pray with the sick person, share the Scriptures on the healing love of God, and witness to what Christ is doing through the anointing. In this way they would prepare the person to be more fully open to the healing grace of the sacrament. Then, having prepared the person for the sacrament, they could join the priest in the celebration.

Other Ways of Praying with the Sick[2]

Praying for physical healing is not, of course, in any way limited to the sacrament of anointing. There are many different forms of praying for healing in the Church. We have para-liturgical healing services. We have "healing teams" in prayer groups and in some parishes. There are pilgrimages to the shrines of Our Lady. Eucharistic ministers, as they bring Holy Communion to the sick and housebound, pray for healing, while a growing number of parishes celebrate a "healing Mass" a few times a year. Some parishes have a parish celebration of the sacrament of anointing for the sick and the elderly; a growing number of people, whether they be priests, religious or laity, now pray spontaneously for any sick person they meet or who may ask for their prayer. Our faith in the healing ministry of Christ in the Church is clearly being restored.

Healing of Agoraphobia

During a parish mission the parish priest asked me to visit a house and pray with a lady called Claire who suffered severely from agoraphobia. She got a complete release from this terrible affliction. Claire describes her condition and healing in this testimony:

> As far back as I can remember, I never had a lot of confidence. A year before my mother died in 1979, I had panic attacks while out shopping, taking the two children to school or even just in the street. Everything I took for granted and loved to do became a nightmare. In fact it was the start of years of Agoraphobia. This fear got so bad I stopped going out. Although sometimes I was able to go with my husband in his car, but always with panic and my heart beating out of my body. There were days when I couldn't go out at all. In fact these days turned into weeks and sometimes months, but the worst was when I started having attacks at home. I would be so frightened of panic

attacks that somebody had to stay with me. Sometimes my husband would take me for a walk at night. I would put my hand on his arm and he would be soaking with perspiration from me. We would only walk 20 or a 100 yards at the most depending on how I felt.

In 1990 our parish priest, Father McGuire, came over to see us. My husband was with me because I was having a bad time. He asked if he could bring over Father McManus the next day as they were having a healing Service at the Church and it was impossible for me to go. The next day I waited for Father. I did not know what to expect as I had prayed for years. When Father came into the living room I thought – "Oh my God, please, please help me." Father McManus put his hands on my head. My husband and Father McGuire also laid hands on me. Father McManus started praying. I don't know what he said as I was crying so much, but I felt hope in me and also a sensation like an electric shock going through me, then a feeling of peace.

The Lord had set her free. She was able to live a normal life. As she said, "I felt strength, peace and joy. I knew I was not alone, the Holy Spirit was guiding me."

Three of us prayed with Claire: her husband, her parish priest and myself. And there was her own heartfelt appeal to the Lord: "Oh my God, please, please help me." I believe that the presence of her husband was all-important for the prayer. He had suffered with her for years. He laid his hands on her with great faith and prayed. The Lord heard his prayer.

A lady who had suffered exactly as Claire, even more acutely, told me about a similar healing. She was hospitalized several times for her agoraphobia. She had panics both inside and outside the house.

Her parish priest persuaded her to go and stand at the door of the church during the parish mission healing service. She told me that she approached the door with great anxiety. Then something happened and she found herself in the body of the church. She joined the crowds on the way up for anointing with blessed oil. She received her blessing and never had another attack of panic. Months after this healing she told me that her greatest joy now was travelling on the London Underground. She could never go down the Underground before her healing.

The interesting thing about this healing is that it seems to have happened as she was standing apart from the congregation, outside the door of the church. Fear of a panic attack prevented her from joining her community as they prayed for healing. The faith of her own parish community seems to have enveloped her, drawn her into the congregation and freed her from the prison of agoraphobia.

Suffering and Healing in the Christian Life

Healing inevitably raises the question of suffering. If we pray for healing, does this mean that suffering is an evil to be avoided? Pamela was suffering pain and privation when the Lord healed her of MS. Fifteen years after the healing she so graphically described in her testimony, she again became seriously ill. In the spring of 1993, she was diagnosed as having cancer and her consultant told her she would not live out the year.

Her parish priest asked her, "Spiritually are you diminished by such extensive suffering?" She responded,

> No, on the contrary, I think I've grown a lot. Quite definitely I've learned a lot about myself and learned to accept a lot in myself that I would have preferred to have left hidden. One of the most powerful things that I have come to realise is to acknowledge and accept my emotions as they arise. Very

often these have been feelings that I would rather not admit to having experienced – loneliness, isolation, fear, doubt, anger, depression, anxiety – they've all been present at one time or another.

She clearly identified the source of her self-acceptance:

Another thing that has developed is my personal relationship with Christ – by telling him exactly how I feel and knowing that I am not only accepted with those feelings, even if they are negative, but loved and cherished for simply being me. I now find Christ to be the closest friend I have – he and I can share everything.[3]

Pamela had discovered what Pope John Paul calls the "Gospel of suffering". At first sight this phrase might seem a contradiction in terms: how can there be a Gospel, a "good news" of suffering? Our society abhors suffering. We want to anaesthetize the whole world against it. We see suffering as something to be avoided at all costs. How can the Pope speak of a Gospel of suffering?

In his encyclical on suffering, John Paul II clearly states that suffering and death are evil, the ultimate consequence of original sin. Christ came to deliver us from this evil. In talking with Nicodemus Jesus said, "For God so loved the world that he gave his only Son, so that everyone who believes in him may not perish but may have eternal life" (Jn 3.16). The ultimate evil would be the definitive loss of eternal life. Pope John Paul writes, "The only-begotten Son was given to humanity primarily to protect man against this definitive evil and against *definitive suffering.*"[4] Christ, in his redemptive work, struck, as the Pope says, the "transcendental roots of evil" which are grounded in sin and death. "He conquers sin by his obedience unto death, and he overcomes death by his Resurrection."[5]

For those who accept his salvation, Christ has destroyed the *eternal* effects of sin, namely the loss of eternal life. But the *temporal* effects of sin, namely suffering and death, remain in this world. The Pope writes:

> Even though the victory over sin and death achieved by Christ in his Cross and Resurrection does not abolish temporal suffering from human life, nor free from suffering the whole historical dimension of human existence, it nevertheless *throws a new light* upon this dimension and upon every suffering: the light of salvation.[6]

Christ enters into the world of suffering. He takes the suffering of the whole world upon himself. As the prophet foretold, "a man of sorrows and familiar with suffering... And yet ours were the sufferings he bore, ours the sorrows he carried... he was pierced through for our faults, crushed for our sins. On him lies a punishment that brings us peace, and through his wounds we are healed" (Isa 53.3-5). Christ entered into the very heart of our world of pain and suffering and by his own suffering and death broke the power of sin and death for each of us.

Because Christ is at the heart of all human suffering we can speak of a "Gospel of suffering". When I said to Pamela that I thought that only those who have found Christ in their suffering can really understand this kind of language, she replied, "Absolutely! But there is no other language to describe what happens to you when you really accept Christ in your sickness and suffering. It is a gospel." Pope John Paul writes: "Down through the centuries and generations it has been seen that in suffering there is concealed a particular power that draws a person interiorly close to Christ, a special grace."[7]

Suffering in itself is not a good thing. But a good thing is concealed in suffering, namely "a particular power that draws a person interiorly close to Christ". When a person is united more intimately to Christ, through this special grace concealed in suffering, the whole nature of suffering is transformed. Indeed, the person can then understand what St Paul meant when he wrote: "I am now rejoicing in my sufferings for your sake, and in my flesh I am completing what is lacking in Christ's afflictions for the sake of his body, that is, the church" (Col 1.24).

Christ's redemption is infinite. We cannot add to it. "But at the same time", Pope John Paul II writes,

> In the mystery of the Church as his Body, Christ has in a sense opened his own redemptive suffering to all human suffering. In so far as man becomes a sharer in Christ's history – to that extent *he in his own way completes* the suffering through which Christ accomplished the Redemption of the world.[8]

We can speak, therefore, of "redemptive suffering". Human suffering in and by itself has no redemptive value; we fight against suffering in every way we can. Human suffering, lovingly united to the suffering Christ, has a "redemptive value". Those who refuse to unite their suffering with Christ on the cross can never recognize this value. It is a value which can be discerned only through the eyes of faith. It is a mystical value. That is why we should always pray for a renewal of faith for the sick person.

Without a renewed and a deepened faith the sick person may not be able to accept what the Church recommends in time of sickness: "The Church exhorts them [the sick] to associate themselves willingly with the passion and death of Christ (see Romans 8.17), and thus contribute to the welfare of the people of God."[9] Indeed, the "sustaining of trust in God" is considered one of the effects of the sacrament of anointing.[10]

Healing in the Spirit

As we approach our ministry to the sick we must be confident that we are bringing the sick into the loving presence of God. We entrust them to God's loving care. This is the very best thing we can do for the sick. We pray confidently for healing, as Christ commands us. To some God grants restored health of mind and body; to others he grants inner healing and new freedom in the Spirit; while to others he grants the interior grace to unite their suffering with the suffering of Christ.

The Church has a message of great hope for the sick. There is multiple healing for body, mind and spirit, because there is healing in the Spirit.

Notes

[1] Decree on the Ministry and Life of Priests, 5.

[2] For a comprehensive and clear exposition of different ways of praying for people see the excellent book by Fr Benedict Heron OSB, *Praying for Healing: The Challenge,* London: Darton, Longman & Todd, 1989.

[3] Cf. *Priests and People,* March 1994, p. 114.

[4] Encyclical on Suffering, 14.

[5] Ibid.

[6] Ibid., 15.

[7] Ibid., 26.

[8] Ibid., 24.

[9] Rite of Anointing, 5.

[10] Ibid., 6.

9

Inner Healing through Forgiveness

Whenever I speak about healing through forgiveness and the unconditional quality of the forgiveness that Christ asks of us, a lively debate normally ensues. What is forgiveness? Whom should we forgive? How can we forgive "the unforgivable"?

Any discussion of forgiveness will very quickly reveal a great variety of opinions within any group. I have found disagreements among priests about the nature of forgiveness. In one discussion, with an international group of priests, one man said that if somebody killed his mother he would probably have to seek revenge before he would even consider forgiveness. Within his culture, he maintained, this would be demanded of him. At a priests' retreat a man objected very strongly to my teaching that unconditional forgiveness included everyone. He said with great conviction, "God may forgive him [a world leader] for what he did to the people but I never will."

The most famous dilemma on forgiveness was posed by Simon Wiesenthal. He was one of the millions of Jews imprisoned in concentration camps during the Second World War. One day he was summoned to a dying SS soldier who wanted to confess his involvement in the murder of Jews and to ask for his forgiveness. Simon listened to the man's appalling story in silence. When the man asked for his forgiveness so that he could die in peace Simon walked away in silence. He concludes his classic account of this encounter this way: "You, who have just read this sad and tragic episode in my life, can mentally change places with me and ask yourself the crucial question, 'What would I have done?'"[1] Should Simon have forgiven the dying man? Could he forgive the dying man in the name of the people whom he had killed?

The Heart of the Gospel

Forgiveness is at the very heart of the Gospel. In the Sermon on the Mount Jesus says, "Love your enemies and pray for those who persecute you" (Mt 5.44) God has forgiven us our sins, and when we contritely turn to him we can begin to live this forgiveness. God forgave us in Christ long before we asked for forgiveness. In responding to God's graciousness to ourselves we embody God's forgiveness in the way we live and relate to others. That is why Jesus says we must forgive seventy times seven (Mt 18.21). We have to extend to those who offend us the forgiveness that we ourselves have received from God. We live lives of "forgiven-ness". As Gregory Jones says in his excellent study:

> Those who are forgiven by Jesus are called to embody that forgiven-ness in the new life signified by communion with Jesus and with other disciples. Indeed that forgiven-ness calls believers to live *penitent* lives that seek to reconstruct human relationships in the service of holiness of heart and life.[2]

Forgiveness, therefore, is primarily a theological concept. It is about what God does for us sinners because of Christ and what the repentant sinner offers to those who sin against him or her in the power of the Spirit. Jesus said to the disciples, just before he ascended, "Thus it is written that the Messiah is to suffer and to rise from the dead on the third day and that repentance and forgiveness of is to be proclaimed in his name to all nations" (Lk 2446-47). Forgiveness, God's forgiveness of us, is the gift of salvation.

Forgiveness originates in God. God forgives us and calls us to live out his forgiveness in a new life, a new way of relating and loving, a converted life. We in our turn, as we live as a forgiven and a forgiving people, offer forgiveness to those who offend us. We can't have God's forgiveness and remain un-repenting people; nor can we be a forgiven but unforgiving people. Forgiveness received from God means forgiveness extended to others. God's forgiveness of us doesn't depend on our willingness to receive. God's forgiveness is offered in and through Christ. Christ has won God's forgiveness for us all. But until we are willing to accept it, we do not experience it. God's forgiveness is prior to our conversion. We don't merit forgiveness by repenting, we accept through repentance the forgiveness which was there all the time. The sign of acceptance is our willingness to embody God's forgiveness in our life. As we embody God's forgiveness, as we begin to live a "forgiven life", our life is transformed in the Spirit and we can now offer to others what we have received from God, namely unconditional forgiveness.

We can embody forgiveness in our relationship with others. We can do this because God gives us his Spirit. The Spirit of Jesus makes alive and active in us the forgiveness which Christ won for us. When we live in the Spirit we live in the power of forgiveness. If there is someone we have to forgive but we feel we can't forgive, even though we know that as forgiven disciples we should forgive, we don't justify our unforgiveness nor do we berate ourselves because of our unforgiveness, rather, we invoke the Spirit to come into our unforgiveness and empower us to forgive. We pray, "Come, Holy Spirit".

Forgiveness is the work of the Spirit. Christ's forgiveness of us comes to us in the Spirit and our forgiveness of others goes to others in the Spirit. St Paul says, "if you live by the Spirit, walk by the Spirit".

Heart of the Church
Jones speaks of "the craft of forgiveness". A craft has to be learned. To become a TV mechanic, you would first have to apprentice yourself to a master mechanic. You would observe the master at

work. You would study the skills of the master, imitate the skills, and eventually make the skills your own. Forgiveness is the craft of living the life we have received from God the Father through the death and resurrection of Jesus, a life which has been given to us in the gift of the Holy Spirit. We have received this life not as isolated individuals but as members of the Church. The Second Vatican Council said:

> At all times and in every nation, anyone who fears God and does what is right has been acceptable to him. (see Acts 10:35). He has, however, willed to make women and men holy and to save them, not as individuals without any bond between them, but rather to make them into a people who might acknowledge him and serve him in holiness.[3]

We stand forgiven before God, not as isolated individuals, but as God's people. When we are greeted at the Eucharist it is not as individuals but as "brothers and sisters". The bond between us which makes us brothers and sisters is the forgiving love of God. The Church is the assembly of the brothers and sisters who have been forgiven by God and who are now called by God to live this forgiveness in his presence. The Council gave us this succinct definition of the Church: "a people made one by the unity of the Father, the Son and the Holy Spirit".[4] As Church we are the people who share in the divine life, a life revealed to us as one of unconditional love and forgiveness. As Church we are a forgiven and a forgiving people. We are called to embody God's divine love and forgiveness in our own lives and to share it with others.

Sharing forgiveness with others is a craft or a skill that we have to acquire. It is a virtue, something that is not an isolated act but a way of life, a character trait of the one who has been forgiven. As Jones says:

Christian forgiveness is at once an expression of a commitment to a way of life, the cruciform life of holiness in which we seek to "unlearn" sin and learn the ways of God, and a means of seeking reconciliation in the midst of particular sins, specific instances of brokenness. In its broadest context, forgiveness is the means by which God's love moves to reconciliation in the face of sin. Hence the craft of forgiveness involves the ongoing and ever-deepening process of sin through forgiveness and learning to live in communion with the Triune God, with one another, and with the whole Creation.[5]

Process

Forgiveness is at the heart of the Gospel but it is also a human process, and, like all processes, it takes time. In recent years psychologists and psychiatrists have been taking the process of forgiveness seriously. Their analysis of the process and stages of forgiveness can be very helpful to those involved in the healing ministry.

From the Christian perspective, forgiveness is primarily a gift of grace, working within our emotional and cognitive processes. The psychological processes at work in forgiveness have been researched by Robert Enright and his team at Wisconsin University for the past fifteen years. Enright is the founder and president of the International Forgiveness Institute at Wisconsin University. In a recent publication he proposes this definition:

Forgiveness is a willingness to abandon one's right to resentment, negative judgment, and indifferent behavior toward one who unjustly injured us, while fostering the undeserved qualities of compassion, generosity, and even love toward him or her. Please note the following points about this definition: 1) The one offended suffered an unjust, perhaps even a deep, hurt from another. 2) The offended willingly chooses to forgive. Forgiving is volitional, not grimly obligatory. 3) The offender's new stance includes affect (overcoming resentment and substituting compassion), cognition (overcoming indifference or the tendency toward subtle revenge with a sense of goodwill). 4) The offended may unconditionally forgive regardless of the other person's current attitudes or behaviors toward the offended, because forgiving is one person's volitional response to another. The sense of forgiveness as wiping away the negative consequences of the offender's injustice and as a merciful reaching out to the offender is consistent with ancient Hebrew, Christian, Islamic, and Confucian texts.[6]

In this definition we see that forgiveness is a choice, it is a change of heart, it is a gift offered to one who doesn't deserve it. In our discussion of forgiveness we will keep these aspects very much in mind. But we will be approaching the process of forgiveness from a different perspective. We will be looking at the healing effect of forgiveness in the one who forgives. In other words, we will be looking at forgiveness not as a gift which the injured offers to the wrongdoer but as a healing, liberating grace which binds up the broken heart of the one who is injured.

Decision

The essential step on the road to forgiveness is the decision to forgive. The hurt person may arrive at this decision only after struggling with the pain of the hurt for some time. In fact, the hurt person will arrive at the decision to forgive when he or she is ready to be healed. If the person is not open to being healed he or she will have no desire to forgive. Instinctively we know that the hurt will not heal so long as we cling on to unforgiveness. The hurt will only deepen as hatred, rage, resentment and bitterness take hold of one's soul. Such negative and destructive sentiments rob the heart of peace.

The fact that we all recognize that hatred, rage and bitterness are bad for one's peace of mind and heart reveals the first ground for forgiveness from a healing point of view, namely our own well-being. God asks us to forgive, not because he wants to impose a burden on us when we have been hurt, but because he knows that the only way to live our new life in the Spirit and have the hurt healed is through forgiveness. "The law of the Lord is perfect, refreshment to the soul" (Ps 19.7). There is refreshment for the soul, for the whole person, in forgiving. Getting rid of bitterness, hatred and rage is a tonic for the whole person. It is not, then, a question of being hurt and then having to forgive in an altruistic spirit without getting anything in return. Rather, it is a question of since I am hurt, I can only be healed through forgiveness. Forgiveness is the gift I offer to the person who has injured me but I cannot offer this gift until I am healed. There is an intimate link between the forgiveness I offer and the healing I experience. Forgiveness can be offered to the wrongdoer only because healing has happened in the heart of the victim. Through forgiveness the broken heart is healed, no matter what the enemy thinks or does.

Forgiveness is not an extra burden, rather it is the way to shed the burden. Forgiveness is not a moral obligation, imposed on us from without. Rather, forgiveness is the inalienable right of the person who has been hurt. No wrongdoer should be allowed to rob us of our right to forgive. As forgiveness is the only path to healing, surrendering our inalienable right to forgive would ensure that we live a life permanently disabled by hatred, rage and vengeance.

Some people have somewhat negatively referred to this approach to forgiveness as "therapeutic forgiveness", as another example of "egoistic faith". Forgiving for what I can get out of it! This view seems to believe that if there is nothing in it for me personally then my actions are purer and more spiritual and Christian. A holistic view, however, has no problem in accepting that God's law reveals what is most wholesome and healing for us. God's law is therapeutic. God doesn't command us to do something that has no bearing on our own personal salvation and human development. God's law of forgiveness is intrinsic to our human development and spiritual welfare. Forgiveness is the only path to true and lasting peace in our world. In the decade of the 1990s 107.8 million people were killed in wars. And at the root of all those conflicts one finds the refusal to forgive. Could we dream that, in the future, statesmen, diplomats and social scientists, as well as religious leaders and theologians, will join forces in educating the people of the world on the healing, liberating and indispensable role of forgiveness in establishing peace and ensuring worldwide solidarity?

Forgiveness, however, is not easy. If forgiveness appears easy, the hurt person has probably gone into denial and pretended the hurt never happened. Forgiveness always means facing the hurt and the consequences that ensued. Forgiveness never engages in denial, nor condoning, nor excusing. Forgiveness always faces reality.

Forgiveness happens within us long before we extend it to the person who hurt us. The hurt has caused pain, resentment and anger; our self-esteem has been threatened; we find ourselves brooding on the hurt and on the perpetrator of the hurt. We become preoccupied with the wrongdoer. In fact, some people spend all their waking moments obsessed with the wrongdoer and re-experiencing the hurt. (The word "resentment" comes from the Latin word *resentire* which means "to feel again"). We may even begin to identify ourselves according to the hurt. Some people sometimes introduce themselves as "I'm John and I am the son of alcoholic parents", or "I'm Rose and I am an incest survivor". The hurt becomes part of the identity, but the false identity. When forgiveness happens within, the person experiences healing of the hurt, the letting go of the false identity, and liberation from the preoccupation with the offender. Now the person can extend in the form of forgiveness the healing that he or she has experienced. Before the person experiences that healing he or she will not be able to offer forgiveness. As William Meninger writes:

> Forgiveness is true freedom. It releases us from being stuck to a cruel event of our past which had stopped the progress of our lives and oriented us to pain and regret. We become free to pursue a better way to real growth and maturity – to become what we should be rather than remain an underdeveloped, frightened child glued to the horror of a past abuse.[7]

What Forgiveness Is Not

True forgiveness, which happens in us and to us, is often slow to come and difficult to receive, but it is made more difficult by the many misconceptions which we have of forgiveness. It will, therefore, be helpful to state clearly what forgiveness is not.

Forgiveness is not *simply a moral or Christian obligation,* imposed from without, it is the *inalienable human right* of those redeemed by Christ. No one can rob a person of this right, because on this right depends a person's healing and wholeness and holiness. Only the person himself or herself can frustrate this inalienable right by choosing not to forgive.

Forgiveness is not *condoning* the wrong, pretending to oneself that it wasn't really all that bad. True forgiveness names the wrong; condoning redefines the wrong and pretends that it was acceptable. Forgiveness is not *excusing.* Excusing means that the person had an excuse and was therefore excusable. If the person was excusable there was nothing to forgive. Forgiving is the opposite of excusing.

It states clearly that what the person did was wrong and that he or she had no excuse. Indeed, the clearest way to say to anyone who has wronged you that he or she was culpable is to say that you forgive. You are saying: "You had no excuse."

Forgiveness is not *tolerating* the wrong. On the contrary, forgiveness says, in the plainest possible way, "What you did was wrong and hurtful and I will not accept it. I refuse to be your victim."

Forgiveness is not *forgetting*. "Forgive and forget" is neither a maxim of wisdom nor a goal in life. A wiser maxim is "forgive and remember", but remember in a new way. We cannot forget the hurt, but forgiveness enables us to remember it without resentment and bitterness. Forgiveness enables us to remember in a learning way. We never forget the hurtful experience; we continue to learn from it. I learn about my own vulnerability, my unrealistic expectations, my proneness to take offence even when no offence was intended. Forgiveness is not *reconciliation*. Reconciliation is what happens between you and the person who hurt you. Forgiveness is what happens within you, which you offer to the one who hurt you as your free gift. Forgiveness is not dependent on what is happening between you and the wrongdoer. You can forgive from the heart even though the person never wants to be reconciled with you. Your forgiveness is never dependent on the other person's willingness to be reconciled. If it were, the healing of your hurt would then depend on the disposition of another person.

Forgiveness is not *letting the offender "off the hook"*. It lets the injured person off the hook of resentment and bitterness. It sets the injured, hurt person free and puts her or him back on the road to wholeness and fulfilled living.

Forgiveness is not *a legal pardon*. You have every right to demand restitution from the person who wronged you. If necessary you can bring him or her before the courts to receive restitution. When Pope John Paul II went to a prison in Rome and forgave Mehmet Ali Agca for trying to kill him he was not calling for his release from prison. Agca was accountable for his actions, for which he was paying the price; and the Pope was accountable for his response to Agca's action and so he forgave. There is no inconsistency between the assailant being sentenced to prison and the Pope forgiving the assailant.

Forgiveness is not *weakness*. It is what a healed person does in the power of the Spirit. Only the healed person can forgive. Forgiveness is saying: "I am now healed of the hurt. I refuse to allow this person to control my life in any way. I offer him or her as a free gift the forgiveness which my healing has made possible." Forgiveness is the strength of Christ forgiving his enemies from the cross.

People who object strongly to forgiveness, like the priest I mentioned at the beginning of this chapter, are really objecting to what forgiveness is not, rather than to what forgiveness is. Who can really object to the one thing that liberates the heart and heals the inner wound?

What Forgiveness Is

Having said what forgiveness is not, let me now try to say what it is. First of all, we have to say that it is the very heart of the Gospel of Christ. Jesus says we must forgive from the heart, seventy times seven. He tells us to "love your enemies and pray for those who persecute you." (Mt 5.44. And St Paul develops this basic Gospel message in Romans:

> Bless those who persecute you; bless and do not curse them… Do not repay anyone evil for evil, but take thought for what is noble in the sight of all. If it is possible, so far as it depends on you, live peaceably with all. Beloved, never

avenge yourselves, but leave room for the wrath of God; for it is written, "Vengeance is mine – I will repay, says the Lord." No, "if your enemies are hungry, feed them; if they are thirsty, give them something to drink; for by doing this you will heap burning coals on their heads." Do not be overcome by evil, but overcome evil with good. (Rom 12.14,17-21))

Psychologist Gerald Jampolsky writes:

From the perspective of Love and Spirit, forgiveness is the willingness to let go of the hurtful past. It is the decision to no longer suffer, to heal your heart and soul. It is the choice to no longer find value in hatred or anger. And it is letting go of the desire to hurt others or ourselves because of something that is already in the past. It is willingness to open our eyes to the light in other people rather than to judge or condemn them.[8]

This comprehensive description of forgiveness emphasizes the words "willingness" and "decision". Remember Enright's definition: "Forgiveness is a willingness to abandon one's right to resentment, negative judgment, and indifferent behavior toward one who unjustly injured us, while fostering the undeserved qualities of compassion, generosity, and even love toward him or her." As psychologists both Enright and Jampolsky focus on the inner states of the mind in the act of forgiving: "willingness to abandon one's right to resentment"; "willingness to let go of the hurtful past"; "decision no longer to suffer"; "choice no longer to find value in hatred or anger"; "letting go of the desire to hurt others"; "willingness to open our eyes to the light in others"; "willingness to foster love for the one who hurt us". The process of forgiveness begins in us with this desire. It may even be "a desire to desire". A person may be in a situation where he or she is saying: "I wish I could even desire to forgive." Even that "desire for the desire" will open the door to the forgiveness process. That's all the desire the Holy Spirit needs to begin his work. That desire is a signal that we want to forgive. We don't want to remain in the prison of hatred or revenge. We recognize that such negative attitudes are bad not just for our spiritual but also for our physical health. Indeed, Jampolsky writes:

> Research into the psychophysiology of human stress has shown us that the thoughts and feelings we hold in our minds are frequently translated into physical symptoms or emotional disorders: anxiety, depression, agitation, poor self-image, headaches, backaches, pains in the neck, stomachaches, and compromised immunity that can make us prone to infection and allergies. It is time to stop attacking our bodies with negative thoughts.[9]

That is why he claims that "forgiveness is the greatest healer of all".

Forgiveness, however, is a process. It is not a one-off act of the will. It takes time and it goes through various stages. Different writers give different names to the various stages a hurt person goes through on the road to forgiveness.[10]

1. *Denial*

Denial is a psychological defence mechanism. The unconscious mind engages in denial as a way of helping the hurt person cope with pain and avoid being overwhelmed by the hurt. A child who is being abused in the home, for instance, will defend itself by this unconscious defence mechanism. When the powerful and significant ones hurt, what can the child do but deny that such things are happening? The adult either denies that the hurting event happened, for example that his or her spouse really had an affair, or denies that it really mattered. He or she minimizes the impact. But, of course, you can see the hurt in what you do and the way you relate. The abused child will, as an adult, engage in abusive behaviour of one kind or another if the wound is not healed. Five years after being cruelly ridiculed and rejected by her boyfriend, Jane maintains that she is over the hurt now and that she will never trust another man. She doesn't connect her lack of trust with her unhealed hurt. Sidney and Suzanne Simon write:

> You may be afraid because once you admit how your were hurt and, even more so, what you have done because of the hurt, you will have to change. You will have to act and react differently from the way you have in the past, and you do not know how to do that. You do not know whether or not you could survive if you did that.[11]

These authors believe that everyone who has been hurt spends some time in the denial stage, and some can remain stuck in this stage for years. Signs of denial would be shrugging off past hurts, claiming that it is "over and done with" or "just so much water under the bridge of life". It is not time but forgiveness that heals hurts. If we have been hurt and if we haven't forgiven and claim that all is well, we are in the stage of denial. We have to name and claim the hurt and blame the person who caused it.

2. Self-blame

This is a very subtle stage in the forgiveness process. What kind of a person would be hurt and then blame himself or herself? The answer seems to be each one of us. When the child is hurt by the parent the child believes that it can avoid further hurt by being a better child. Children often blame themselves for the divorce of their parents. If only they had been better children their parents would not have fought so much! The adult frequently uses phrases such as "if only". If only I had taken the other road, or if only I had left ten minutes earlier, or if only I had never taken that new job, or if only I had made it up right away.

In the stage of self-blame we tend subtly to take responsibility for what happened, even though it wasn't our fault. This can give us a certain security for the future. If the pain was our own fault, then we can avoid it in the future by acting differently. We have to say without any equivocation that if one spouse is unfaithful to the other it is not the faithful spouse's fault; if a parent abuses a child it is not the child's fault; if a person is mugged on the way home it is not his or her fault for not taking a different route or leaving ten minutes earlier. Don't blame the victim. We blame the person who inflicted the hurt. That person, and he or she alone, was responsible.

3. *The victim stage*

When you have been hurt you have been victimized. In the stage of denial you will deny victimization. But once having broken out of denial and stopped blaming yourself, you will become very aware of what has happened to you. Now you will be able to say that you have been wronged and that your "enemies" had no right to do what they did. At this stage you may well begin to wallow in your pain, even boast about how your life has been destroyed. You become excessively aware of those who have wronged you and you live every day in their shadow. You pass from having been victimized into the state of being the victim. You can whine and moan and groan and fill the room with negative feelings and energy. You want to talk about nothing but your own pain. This can be a healing stage because it places the blame where it belongs, namely on the culprit. But a person stuck in the victim stage sees his or her hurt at the centre of the universe. "There was no hurt like my hurt!" The choice the person has to make is whether he or she wants to remain a victim for ever.

4. *The indignation stage*

This is the stage of anger. You hear yourself saying very clearly, "what they did was wrong and destructive and they had no right to do it to me". Denial and self-blame give way to righteous indignation.

You are no longer a victim. You have made the decision that you will not remain a victim of the person's injustice for another moment. You will get on with your life. This indignation at what happened to you energizes you for action. It releases your healthy anger from repression. Many of us deny our anger or unconsciously repress it. We may even believe that anger in itself is bad or sinful. But anger is a good emotion. Anger directed at vengeance is bad; anger directed at injustice is good. Going through this stage of anger and indignation is a necessary part of the journey towards forgiveness. But, of course, we can also get stuck in the indignation stage. Having got in touch with our anger we then hold on to it and refuse to let go. If this happens healing doesn't happen and we end up angry people. Sometimes hurt people, who have discovered their anger, can remain stuck in it for years. Their anger becomes aggression and their behaviour unacceptable even to their friends. They end up not only hurt but friendless.

5. *The survivor stage*

The survivor begins to make the discovery that despite the hurts and the rejections life is beginning to have a new meaning and purpose. Life is no longer defined and prescribed by the hurts of the past; life is open to the future and it is up to oneself to make a good future. The person discovers that life is good and worth living. "For one thing, in the survivor stage you spend more and more time *looking ahead toward health instead of back toward your pain.*" [12] You begin to realize that despite everything that happened to you, you are still alive, still in charge of your own life, and now wanting to get your life back under your own control. You recognize that living in denial, or self-blame, or indignation, or victimhood was not a healthy lifestyle. The hurts and wounds of the past were real, but they belong to the past. You don't have to bring them into the future. The survivor draws a line in the sand and proclaims that the resentments, grudges, bitterness and unforgiveness will not pass. They will not be part of the future which is opening up.

Although you may have *thought* this before, in the survivor stage you actually *do* it. After years of merely responding to the people and circumstances that you happened to encounter, you take back the reins that you handed over to fate and play an active role in determining your own destiny. You become an actor instead of a reactor, a player in the game of life rather than a spectator watching from the sidelines while life passes you by".[13]

6. *The integration stage*

The integration stage happens very often without your noticing. You wake up one morning and realize that the miracle has happened, you have let go of the pain and the resentment and the rage. You have forgiven. Something has happened inside you. C.S. Lewis wrote to his friend Malcolm: "Last week while at prayer, I suddenly discovered – or felt as if I did –that I had forgiven someone I had been trying to forgive for over 30 years."[14] Forgiveness happens within you before you can offer it to others. At the stage of integration it is not a question of trying or forcing yourself to forgive. Rather, it is the discovery that in some mysterious way you have already forgiven. All the emotional baggage that bound you to the past hurt has been jettisoned. You can look back at the hurt with new insight As Rowan Williams writes: "If forgiveness is liberation, it is also a recovery of the past in hope, a return of the memory, in which what is potentially threatening, destructive, despair-inducing, in the past is transfigured into a ground of hope."[15] As I accept my past, and everything that has happened to me in the past, I can accept myself just as I am in the present in a new and healing way. In accepting yourself unconditionally in the present you can also accept the hurts of the past that contributed in their own way to how you are in the present.

The truth is that you were always more than your hurt. At the integration stage you discover that "more" and, in a way that would seem to be totally foolish to a person in the victim stage, you can be grateful. You no longer try to totally banish the person who hurt you from your life. You now accept that that person has had a role in your life history and you want to keep your history intact. In fact, you are now so healed within that you are ready for reconciliation with the person who hurt you if that person is ready to reciprocate. Your forgiveness does not depend on the reconciliation. Your forgiveness is now unconditional. Your forgiveness is something that has happened within you and the fact that the other person is not willing to be reconciled in no way limits or restricts the quality of your forgiveness. Now, even if he or she tells you to "stuff your forgiveness" you are still forgiving. The reason should now be obvious. Forgiveness is not what he or she deserves, nor is it a duty that you owe or a moral obligation that you are under. It is your inalienable right as a person to protect your personal dignity as a redeemed child of God and have your inner wound healed. Philip McGraw sums it up well when he writes:

> The reason I believe forgiveness is such an important element is that, without it, you are almost inevitably destined to a life marred by anger, bitterness, and hatred. Those emotions only compound the tragedy. You are the one who pays the price by carrying the negative emotions with you, allowing them to contaminate every element of your current life. Forgiveness is not a feeling that you must passively wait to wash over you. Forgiveness is a choice, a choice that you can make to free yourself from the emotional prison of anger, hatred, and bitterness. I am not saying that the "choice" is an easy one, only that it is a necessary one.[16]

Having lived through the various stages of forgiveness we recognize that the healing began with our decision to forgive. That was the moment of grace. It may have been a long, painful journey. But in the end it was a liberation and it brought healing integration.

People have often commented on the fact that the road to forgiveness is not a straight one. You don't live through or walk through the six stages we have identified without slipping back. You may one day be in the indignation stage and the next day you are back in the victim stage. Or one day you seem to be working your way through the victim stage and the next day you have regressed to the self-blame stage. This regression to an earlier stage is to be expected. The helpful thing about identifying the stages is that when regression happens you can recognize where you are. When you seem to be making no progress, you can recognize what is going on. As long as you haven't decided to stop you are still on the journey towards forgiveness. And, if you remain journeying, you will arrive.

Someone may say: "You have outlined a purely natural or psychological process. Where is the grace of God in all this?" Precisely within the process. The grace of God doesn't act on us from without; it works from within us, from within our psychological laws and processes. God created those laws and processes for our wholeness and growth. Of course, as we live through the stages of forgiveness with faith and prayer, and as we bring our inner wound to the Lord for healing, the forgiveness process will, I believe, evolve much faster. The person of deep faith and love may live through all the stages in a relatively short space of time. Gordon Wilson, whom we met in Chapter 5, forgave the members of the IRA on the very night that his daughter was killed by their bomb. Many a person in that tragic situation would have spent the rest of his or her life in resentment, bitterness and rage. Such forgiveness is extraordinary, but it isn't rare. Many of the families who have lost loved ones through the violence in Northern Ireland seem to have that same grace of forgiveness. They appeal for no revenge and they offer forgiveness. They live through the stages of forgiveness very quickly. They have received the gift of inner healing and peace. On the other hand there are those who have been injured or lost loved ones through the violence whose wounds have never healed. Their only comfort seems to be in making certain that they will never forgive.

Forgiveness begins with the desire to forgive and none of the healing, integration and liberation that forgiveness brings will begin to happen without that desire. The desire is the prompting of grace. A person may be intellectually convinced that the best thing to do is to embark on the road to forgiveness but may have no desire to do so. He or she should, at that stage, ask for the grace. Jesus came "to bind up the brokenhearted" (Isa 61.1). He does that through giving us the power and the grace to forgive. We can, therefore, confidently ask for the grace at each of the six stages we have outlined. Even when the hurt person is wallowing in self-pity in the victim stage he or she can still whisper a prayer and ask for healing and wholeness and a better life. The grace of forgiveness restores our inner power and we are once again in control of our own lives.

Reframing

The grace of forgiveness helps us to rediscover the humanity of those who have afflicted us. The deep hurt may be responsible for our demonizing them, casting them out into outer darkness, expelling them from the face of the earth. We can deny all kinship with them. So long as we de-humanize them in our own minds we will never move towards healing and forgiveness. The first step is to discover again the kinship of our common humanity. Despite what they have done they are no less human than we are. We have to change the way we see them. This is called "reframing". Joanna North writes:

> Enright and his colleagues have described reframing as a process whereby the wrongdoer is viewed *in context* in an attempt to build up a complete picture of the wrongdoer and his actions. Typically, this involves understanding the pressures that the wrongdoer was under at the time of the wrong and an appreciation of the wrongdoer's personality as a result of his particular developmental history.[17]

Reframing helps us to separate the wrongdoer from the wrong he or she has committed. When someone does something bad it is a natural instinct to see only the bad and to see the person as a "bad person". But there is more to the person than the "bad" that he or she has done. We don't confuse the sinner with the sin; we don't identify the wrongdoer with the wrong. We separate the person from the evil he or she does. The Christian maxim is that we hate the sin but not the sinner. We condemn the wrong but forgive the wrongdoer.

Reframing enables us to see more in the wrongdoer than the wrong. We see our common humanity. As long as we deny the wrongdoer's humanity we will be in pain. Lewis Smedes says:

> The original wallop is only the beginning of the pain. There is a reflex pain that comes hard on the heels of the original blow – the reactive pain of frustrated fury. Fuelled by our resentment, our memory tucks this pain in an inside pocket of our spirits where it fattens on our happiness. It becomes a pain that swells in the spirit long after the original injury. This is the pain that forgiving was invented to heal.[18]

The process of reframing enables us to see the person in a different light. Reframing is the result of the "cognitive" change that Enright identified in his definition. Forgiveness, through reframing, enables us to see good in the other, despite the harm he or she did to us.

Smedes outlines five steps to undertake before we even try to forgive:

> **Think:** What really happened? It takes time to clarify this for oneself.
>
> **Evaluate:** Was the hurtful action or word really intended? Was it an uncharacteristic response from a person who was normally friendly? Maybe it was an accident? Or was it a misunderstanding? Before you think of forgiving you have

to be clear about the nature of the hurt, the intention behind the hurt, and the deliberation in causing the hurt.

Talk: Get a second opinion or even a third opinion on what you think happened and on why it happened and what you should do about it. Talking the matter over with a friend may bring all the healing you need.

Feel: Get in touch with your emotions. This takes time. It is best done in silence, on a long walk, or in a quiet church or place of prayer. Accept and honour each emotion you get in touch with – anger, resentment, fury, rage, and so on. Don't reject any emotion.

Pray: Now bring all your hurt emotions to God your Father and tell him exactly how you feel. If you feel revengeful, talk to God about it; if you feel full of hatred and bitterness, pour it all out before the crucified Lord. And ask the Holy Spirit for the will to do God's will, to liberate and heal yourself of the pain and the hurt by forgiving. God gives us the command to forgive because he wants us to live in freedom, healed of all our wounds.

The Dalai Lama writes:

A few years back, a Tibetan monk who had served about eighteen years in a Chinese prison in Tibet came to see me after his escape to India. I knew him from my days in Tibet and remembered last seeing him in 1959. During the course of that meeting I had asked him what he felt was the biggest threat or danger while in prison. I was amazed at his answer. It was extraordinary and inspiring. I was expecting him to say something else: instead he said that what he most feared was losing his compassion for the Chinese.[19]

Compassion was what he valued most highly in himself. To lose compassion for the Chinese would be a much greater loss than losing his freedom for eighteen years in jail. The loss of compassion would have robbed him of his sense of integrity. Compassion is the heart of forgiveness, and the heart of the Gospel. Jesus even says to us: "Be compassionate as your heavenly Father is compassionate" (Lk 6.35). The grace of forgiveness is truly divinizing because it makes us as compassionate as our heavenly Father. God created us in his own image and he wants us to manifest his image in our compassion and love embodied in forgiveness. As we embody forgiveness, full of compassion and love for the enemy, we become like God. The enemy may remain hostile, but we are being transformed by compassion and love.

In praying with people for the grace of forgiveness we have to be patient. We try to discern what stage the hurt person is at and then we accept that stage and honour how the person is feeling in that stage. But accepting and honouring doesn't mean that we don't challenge the person to move forward. We may have to say, "I know you feel very much the victim right now but you will not remain a victim for the rest of your life. God will heal you and you will forgive." By staying patiently with hurting people, helping them to recognize where they are hurting and keeping them open to the great mystery of God's forgiving love poured into their hearts, you can gently lead them along the path of forgiveness. Then one day they wake up and discover that they have forgiven.

Notes

[1] Simon Wiesenthal, *The Sunflower: On the Possibilities and Limits of Forgiveness,* New York: Schocken Books, 1997, p. 98.

[2] L. Gregory Jones, *Embodying Forgiveness: A Theological Analysis,* Grand Rapids, MI: Eerdmans, 1995, p.121.

[3] Constitution on the Church, 9.

[4] Constitution on the Church, 4.

[5] Jones, *Embodying Forgiveness,* p. 230.

[6] Robert Enright & Joanna North (eds.) *Exploring Forgiveness*, Maddison, WI: University of Wisconsin Press, 1998, p. 47.

[7] William Meninger, *The Process of Forgiveness*, New York: Continuum, 1999, p. 36.

[8] Gerald Jampolsky, *Forgiveness: The Greatest Healer of All,* Hillsboro, OR: Beyond Words Publishing, 1999, p. 17.

[9] Ibid. p. 57.

[10] Sidney B. Simon and Suzanne Simon, *Forgiveness: How to Make Peace with your Past and Get on with your Life,* New York: Warner, 1991, pp. 77-240; Meninger, *Process of Forgiveness,* pp. 47-72; Beverly Flanigan, *Forgiving the Unforgivable,* New York: Macmillan, 1992, pp. 71-186. I am following the stages outlined by Simon and Simon.

[11] Simon and Simon, *Forgiveness,* p. 80.

[12] Ibid., p. 182.

[13] Ibid.

[14] C.S. Lewis, *Letters to Malcolm: Chiefly on Prayer,* New York: Harcourt, Brace and World, 1964, p. 106.

[15] See Jones, *Embodying Forgiveness,* p. 177.

[16] Philip C. McGraw, *Self Matters: Creating Your Life from the Inside Out*, London: Free Press, 2001, p. 282.

[17] Enright and North, *Exploring Forgiveness,* p. 26.

[18] Lewis B. Smedes, *The Art of Forgiving,* New York: Ballantine Books, 1996, p. 18.

[19] See Wiesenthal, *The Sunflower,* p. 130.

10

Healing Services

The healing service is a notable new expression of the healing ministry that has been developed in some parishes in the last twenty years. This is a para-liturgical service consisting of reading of the word of God, teaching on the word, prayers for healing based on the word, and finally individual blessing and anointing with blessed oil. The healing service provides the optimum opportunity for teaching on the nature of Christian healing. Within the context of the service, through the Scripture, teaching and prayers, the meaning of Christian healing becomes clear.

In fact the healing service makes the meaning of Christian healing much clearer than even the most eloquent lecture. For example, during a week on the healing ministry which I had organized at Hawkstone Hall in 1978 Francis McNutt was the speaker. Francis was a very eloquent speaker, charismatically alive, and a good theologian. A large group of people, including bishops, priests and several doctors, attended the conference. One doctor, a member of the Lourdes Medical Bureau, was having great difficulties with Francis' approach to healing. He was challenging him at every opportunity, pointing out the medical explanations that were possible for the many instances of healing which Francis mentioned. The rest of us were getting a little restless with his constant interruptions. Then we all travelled to a large parish church in Birmingham where Francis conducted a healing service. The church was packed and Francis and his team prayed with everyone. The doctor followed Francis throughout the service, observing in detail everything that was going on. When we reassembled the following morning for the first session, even before Francis began the doctor was on his feet.

He began by reminding Francis that he had been challenging many of his statements throughout the week. Then he said: "If you had begun the week with the healing service you conducted last night I would have had no difficulties. Your service answered all my problems." In the service he saw that Francis was not trying to be a doctor or a psychiatrist but a preacher of the word of God, calling people to put their trust in God's plentiful redemption.

Talking about healing is one thing, praying to God for healing is quite another thing. If we remain simply on the level of talking, healing becomes just another speculative subject, something to discuss, something that may be of interest to a few people but which will never grip large numbers. About sixty people attended Francis' week on the healing ministry; about two thousand came to his healing service. The healing service combines teaching with praying, talking about healing with worshipping God, thinking about the healing of memories and relationships with the acknowledgement of one's own sins and one's need for God's forgiveness. The healing service is an act of worship; it is a confession of one's own sinfulness; it is an acknowledgement of how we have failed to live by every word that comes from the mouth of God.

Structure of Healing Service

In my healing services I pray for healing in four areas: memories, relationships, spiritual healing and physical healing. I follow four steps in praying in each area:

(1) I read a short Scripture passage.
(2) I give a short teaching on the passage, applying it to the specific area of healing.
(3) I lead some spontaneous prayer for healing in that area.
(4) The whole congregation responds in a short song of praise.

This format helps to create a listening, worshipping community, focused on the healing presence of Christ and the power of his word. I use this format because I believe that all healing comes through hearing the word of God and acting on it. Jesus says that we don't live by bread alone "but by every word that comes from the mouth of God" (Mt 4.4). In every situation in which we find ourselves in life there is a word of God to live by. If we live by that word we will have what Jesus promised, namely "life in abundance" (John 10.10). If we don't live by that word we will have an impoverished life and we will know bitterness and disillusionment. I find it necessary to expound on this at the beginning of the healing service. I say that we have come to hear the word of God and to put it into practice. Jesus said: "Blessed are those who hear the word of God and obey it" (Lk 11.28). How do we keep the word in our heart? And if we are keeping the word in our heart, what is the word doing there?

The most important teaching we can impart to people about the healing ministry is that all healing comes through hearing the word of God and acting on it. Healing is not a magic touch or a magical prayer. Healing comes about when the person opens his or her heart to the word and the promise of God and then acts on the word. By hearing the word we are filled with faith; by acting on the word we receive God's promise. There should be a proclamation of the word in every healing service and in every healing prayer. We have to hear again and recall that God's word is creative. As the letter to the Hebrews says, "God's word is alive and active" (Heb 4.12). As we proclaim the word in the healing service the word becomes alive and active. The word accomplishes what it says. The word of God promises peace; the word of God brings peace. The word of God promises healing; the word of God brings healing. The celebration of the word of God, the prayerful hearing of and devout responding to the word of God, are the very heart of the healing service. Whatever healing happens during the healing service is effected by the hearing of the word of God. It is not the word of the one conducting the service that brings the healing. It is God's word proclaimed through the Scripture and the teaching of whoever leads the service. Of course, the word must be proclaimed with faith and expectation, with devotion and reverence. And it must be heard with the same dispositions. Jesus talked about people who had "ears but could not hear, eyes but could not see". If we don't listen to the word of God at the healing service I doubt very much if we will receive any blessing. If the blessing comes through the hearing of the word, how can we be blessed if we are not receiving the word through prayerful listening?

As we gather for the healing service it is good to remind ourselves that long before we got to the service we were being prayed for in the heart of heaven by Christ himself and we were being prayed in by the Holy Spirit in our own hearts. In the penitential rite at the beginning of Mass we often say to Christ: "You plead for us at the right hand of the Father". That is Jesus' constant ministry for us in the presence of his Father. He is interceding for us. As the letter to the Hebrews says, he is now "in the presence of God on our behalf" (Heb 9.24). When we come to pray, and especially when we come to pray for healing, it is good to remind ourselves that since long before we got to our prayer Jesus and the Holy Spirit have been praying for us. All we have got to do is to relax into their prayer and allow their prayer to lift us up to God. The healing service can create the atmosphere where it becomes easier for us to let go of all our worries and anxieties and rest in God.

Healing of Memories

The first area of healing I pray for is the healing of memories. Memory is a great gift of God. Through memory we can recall everything that has ever happened to us. Every single experience of life is registered in our memory. Memory is the original computer. Whenever we wish we can recall some past event of our life and make it present to us now, sometimes vividly present. And there are times when the past remains vividly present in our memories even when we are trying to forget. Something bad or painful has happened. Before we are awake for five minutes it all comes rushing back into our consciousness. The computer of memory has no delete button. We cannot simply forget.

How do we live by the word of God with regard to these past events which keep disturbing the present? And what is the word of God with regard to the past? The word I build the healing of memories around is taken from Psalm 103, which begins: "Bless the Lord, O my soul, and all that is within me, bless his holy name. Bless the Lord, O my soul, and do not forget all his benefits." In this psalm the Holy Spirit directs us to bless God with all that is within us, that is with everything that has ever happened to us in our whole life. There is no distinction made between the good and the bad things, the painful and the joyful things, the successes and the failures. Everything within, all our past life experience, has now only one thing to do and that is to bless God. Our life experience within us is saying something to God. It is either blessing or cursing. If there is some part of my life experience which is not yet blessing, which instead of saying "God bless it" is saying "God damn it", which is cursing, then, of course, I will not be at peace in that area. And that memory of that past experience will be painful. When I encounter this painful memory, when I want to have this painful memory healed, I have only one option and that is to live by the word of God that says "all that is within me, bless".

The healing service provides us with a grace-filled opportunity to begin thanking God even for the bad things in life. We have the support of the community; we are worshipping God together; our spirits are uplifted by music and singing; and the proclamation of God's word and the teaching strengthen us to face these painful realities not with a curse but with a blessing. The teaching on the need to thank God is vital in the healing service. We are not just passive recipients of healing. We are active collaborators with God in our own healing. Our collaboration takes the form of living by the word that says "all that is within me bless". If we don't live by this word we are refusing to collaborate in our own healing and the painful memory will remain unhealed.

I lead the congregation in this kind of prayer for the healing of memories:

> Lord, we thank you for every moment of existence. We praise you Lord, for every moment of joy and happiness and we thank you too, Lord, for every moment of sadness and failure. Lord Jesus, make us truly grateful. We thank you, Lord, for all the times when things went wrong, for the times when despite our best efforts, hopes and prayers things didn't work out as we had hoped. Lord Jesus, make us truly grateful. We thank you, Lord, for every disappointment and every frustration, for all the sad and the bad things that have happened. Lord Jesus, make us truly grateful.

This type of simple prayer will now have focused the congregation on gratitude to God for their whole past life. Bad memories will now be coming into consciousness. This is a time for silence. I invite the congregation to enter into the silence of their heart and simply offer to God whatever has come to mind. And I remind them too that Christ and the Holy Spirit are now praying with them and for them. Even if they feel that at this moment they cannot bring themselves to say "thanks be to God" for something in the past they can ask these two great, divine intercessors to thank the Father for them. This always helps people to open their heart in trust in God, take the leap of faith and say "thanks be to God". As they open to the grace of gratitude they discover within themselves a new power to praise God. And, as they enter into praise, the painful memories are healed. C.S. Lewis put it well: "Praise is inner health made audible." As the person with the painful memory really enters into praise, living deeply the word that says "all that is within me, bless", he or she experiences healing. The painful memory is gone and in its stead there is now a grateful memory.

It is surprising the number of people who seek healing for a painful memory of the past but who are unwilling to let go of it and say "thanks be to God". The memory is painful; they don't want the disturbance it causes; yet they refuse to live by the word of God that directs them to pray "all that is within me, bless God's holy name". I was puzzled by this reluctance for a long time. Then one day I saw clearly that people are reluctant to say "thanks be to God" for some past, painful event because they know that the moment they say "thanks be to God" for it they can no longer moan and groan about it. They want to be rid of the pain without surrendering their moans and groans. Of course, what gets rid of the pain also gets rid of the moans and groans. That is their dilemma. Wouldn't it be great to get healing without having to change, without having to live by the word of God?

The healing service helps us to face our own past sins and say "thanks be to God" for them. Some people say that what they did was so bad that they couldn't possibly thank God for it. How can we say thanks to God for our past sins? After we have asked God's pardon for our sins, maybe for the hundredth time, what do we say to God about them? What does the Church say to God about the sin of Adam, that original sin which is at the source of all our own sins? At the Easter Vigil the Church sings: "O happy fault, O necessary sin of Adam, which gained for us so great a Redeemer!" If the Church can praise God even for the sin of Adam, we too can surely thank God for all the sins for which we have repented long ago. This teaching in the healing service helps people to look back over their whole life, and no matter what has happened, to humbly say a big "thanks be to God". Try it for yourself.

The healing service also helps us praise God for the sins others have committed against us. These bad things of the past come under the command "all that is within me, bless God's holy name". In praising God for them I am not saying, "I am glad they happened" but I am saying that God was present, even in those bad things, and that God will bring my ultimate good out of those bad things. We cannot change the past. But we can change the way we remember the past. We can remember either resentfully or gratefully, with bitterness or with peace, with acceptance or with rejection. The healing of memories enables us to remember in a grateful way. It makes it possible for us to accept the past without bitterness and to place the whole past in the hands of God. That is where it belongs. The healing service helps us to leave everything in God's hands.

Healing of Relationships

The next area I pray for in the healing service is the healing of relationships. This healing also comes through living by the word of God. The word that God speaks to us about those who wrong us is "forgive seventy times seven". In the healing service we have the opportunity to clarify the many misunderstandings that people have in their minds about forgiveness. I briefly review some of the misunderstandings that I mentioned in the previous chapter on forgiveness.

People praying for the healing of painful relationships will be at different stages in the healing process. Jesus says that we must "forgive from the heart". The healing service helps us to face those who hurt us in our hearts, look at what they did to us in the presence of God, ask God to forgive them and ask God to give us the power to forgive them . Many people have a struggle on their hands at this point. They don't want the pain of resentment, bitterness and unforgiveness, and yet they find it hard to let go and forgive. As the prayer progresses their hearts are touched by grace, the pain is healed and they come into the power to forgive. They discover in the presence of God that they have been healed of deep pain and now they are able to forgive. As they acknowledge their own sinfulness in the presence of God they are able to accept that others too are sinful. They share with those who wronged them a common sinful humanity.

For the healing of relationships I lead the congregation in this kind of spontaneous prayer:

> Lord, we thank you for the gift of so many brothers and sisters with whom we have the privilege of sharing our life. Lord, we ask your pardon for the many ways in which we refuse to share. Lord Jesus, our divine healer, heal within us everything that refuses to love and forgive as you do. Jesus, heal our arrogance and our pride. Lord, heal our proneness to sit in judgement and find fault. Lord, heal our inability to forgive. Lord, we want to go out now in the power of your Spirit and offer unconditional forgiveness to everyone who has hurt us. (I ask the congregation to name the persons in their hearts and say, "Lord, in your Spirit I now forgive Mary and Joe etc.")

In the silence of the forgiveness prayer, great healing happens. Normally those whom we have to forgive are the ones we love. As a means of helping the congregation face these I often mention a number by name. Parents have to forgive their children; children, even sixty-year-olds, have to forgive their parents; husbands and wives have to forgive each other; brothers and sisters have to forgive one another. Very often we have to forgive other significant people in our lives like teachers, priests, colleagues at work, best friends.

Sometimes too we may have to forgive people who may be strangers to us but have wronged us in some way. The parent whose child may have been killed in a car accident will have to forgive the driver, or the person whose house may have been burgled will have to forgive the thief. (This, as explained in the last chapter, does not mean offering the thief a legal pardon.) The worshipping silence, the prayer, the praise, help the hurt person to open up the hurt to God's healing love and come into freedom. Having offered forgiveness, I then ask the people to pray that God will fill those whom they have forgiven with the Holy Spirit. The vision of the person being filled with the Holy Spirit is very healing in itself. I can now contemplate my "enemy" being blessed with God's Spirit. That is a sure sign that I have forgiven. After a healing service people are always very grateful that they were led through a prayer of forgiveness.

Spiritual Healing

The third area of healing which I pray for in a healing service is spiritual healing. This term covers the area of my own weaknesses and sinfulness. How do I live by the word of God with regard to these? I like to read God's word to St Paul: "My grace is sufficient for you" (2 Cor 12.9). Whatever the weakness, or whatever our strengths for that matter, we depend entirely on God's grace. The healing service helps us to relate to our own weaknesses in a gentle and accepting way. St Paul says: "The Spirit helps us in our weakness" (Rom 8:26). The Holy Spirit wants to be at the very heart of our weakness. We tend to exclude the Spirit from our weaknesses. We may invite the Spirit to come into what we consider our strengths, into those areas where we are trying to be good and helpful to others, areas where we are keeping the commandments. But in those areas where we fail, the areas of moral struggle and weakness, we don't instinctively invite the Spirit in. Yet that is where the Holy Spirit wants to be, at the very heart of our weakness.

In response to God's word, "my grace is enough for you: for power is at full stretch in weakness", St Paul says: "So, I will boast all the more gladly of my weaknesses, so that the power of Christ may dwell in me" (2 Cor 12.9). In this prayer for spiritual healing we have to imitate St Paul and boast about our weaknesses. We begin by repenting of our sins and asking pardon. Then we invite the Holy Spirit to come into the area of our greatest weakness, whether that weakness is emotional or moral. I like to address this kind of prayer, at this point, to the Spirit:

> Holy Spirit, you are the light of God in our darkness; Holy Spirit, you are the strength of God in our weakness; Holy Spirit, you are the holiness of God in our sinfulness; Holy Spirit, you are the wisdom of God in our foolishness and we worship you. Come, Holy Spirit, into the very heart of our weakness; Holy Spirit, come into every area of addiction in our lives (addiction to alcohol, gambling, drugs, pornography, self-abuse of any kind); Holy Spirit, come, fill our hearts with your peace and love; come, Holy Spirit, and sanctify us with your holiness, enlighten us with your light, guide us with your wisdom and confirm us with your strength.

As the congregation enters into this invocation of the Holy Spirit a great peace normally descends. We are no longer judging or condemning ourselves. We are accepting that we are weak and sinful people and that we depend entirely on God's gift of the Spirit. This is a gentle way of relating to our own weaknesses. There is no point in berating ourselves for our weaknesses. Self-condemnation changes nothing. The only thing that can change us is the invocation of the Holy Spirit. We accept our weaknesses and we live the word that "my grace is enough for you".

This invocation of the Holy Spirit is very healing for those who are struggling with great moral or addictive weaknesses. No matter what the situation may be, no matter how hopeless the case may seem from the human point of view, we can always say with complete confidence "Come, Holy Spirit". A person who may feel very far from God because of lifestyle or weaknesses needs to be encouraged to open his or her heart to God and call confidently on the Spirit to come. The good news in all our difficulties is: "nothing is impossible to God" (Lk 1.37).

Physical Healing

Finally in the healing service I pray for physical healing. The congregation have been led through three stages of inner healing: the healing of memories, the healing of relationships and spiritual healing. They are now well aware that physical healing is only one type of healing and maybe not the most important type. Still, people always come to the healing service with physical sicknesses and pain. And we pray for their healing.

Jesus asked his disciples to lay their hands on the sick and pray for them. I often ask the congregation to do just that, to lay their right hand on the shoulder of the person sitting next to them and pray for the healing of that person. The first time I asked a congregation to do that I was amazed and delighted with the response. A reverential silence descended on all. When they do this people forget about themselves and their own needs and go out in prayer to their neighbour. For many it will be the first time they have prayed in this way, and for the vast majority, if not all, it is a good and prayerful experience. This takes the focus away from the one who is leading the service. Christ himself is present in the congregation. It is in and through the community that he now heals his people.

The healing service, which we really should call a service of prayer for healing, is a celebration of the word of God and provides people with an experience of the power of God. Faith, as St Paul says, "does not rest on human wisdom, but on the power of God" (1 Cor 2.5). If faith is not resting on the power of God, God becomes a very distant Father, if not just a vague idea. People need to know the presence of God; they need to experience his power in their own lives and witness his Spirit at work in the Church.

Praying for healing is the manifestation of the power of God, because God alone can heal. The preacher who proclaims the healing love of God, but refuses to pray for healing is not really bearing witness to the message. Preaching is always more than words. Preaching must be a witness to the message and a demonstration of the truth of the message. The healing service provides a good opportunity for preaching the Gospel with power and complete conviction. There is a very intimate relationship between preaching conversion and praying for healing. As one person put it, "preaching without healing is powerless, healing without preaching is pointless." Healing is always a sign of the love of God inviting us into his Kingdom.

Anointing with the Oil of Gladness

I conclude the healing service with an anointing with blessed oil. This blessed oil is often called "the oil of gladness". That is an appropriate name because it symbolizes the joy that the Holy Spirit gives. People return to their homes glad in heart. They have opened their whole lives to the Spirit; they have surrendered their weaknesses to God and they have invited Christ to send his Spirit into the heart of their weaknesses. God hears that prayer and blesses his people with peace and joy.

During an ecumenical retreat in a top-security prison in London the healing service was a most blessed occasion. Men with very bitter memories found deep peace in the Lord. One prisoner described the anointing in a letter to his parish priest:

The final part was the anointing with the oil of gladness. Yes, we were anointed with the oil of gladness on the forehead and the hands. Each of the four chaplains plus Father Jim performed the anointing as lines of men went up to be anointed. We asked for special intentions and for healing in ourselves and for others. I prayed for a moment or two with the chaplain and returned to my place. Hymns of praise and thanksgiving were being sung throughout. It was beautiful.

This healing service was a preparation for the final session with the prisoners on the following evening. The same prisoner described the occasion:

How can I express in words the experience of Sunday evening? We gathered and prayed for the gift of the Holy Spirit in words and singing continuously. It was an experience of great joy. We prayed collectively for the gifts of the Spirit for ourselves. Then we went individually to be prayed with. There was a continuous stream of people going up. Everyone was joyfully singing or praying. I could see great joy on the faces of everyone. It was out of this world.

The blessing with oil and the prayer for the release of the Spirit have that effect on people. They come forward with great expectation and they are not disappointed. Those prisoners, many of whom were serving life sentences for very serious crimes, had a profound experience of the healing presence of the Lord through the anointing. I have often asked myself what I would have done for those men if I hadn't conducted the healing service on the Saturday and prayed for the release of the Spirit on the Sunday. Words alone would not have brought them into that experience of the joy of the Spirit.

The blessing with the oil is a simple blessing. It is not a sacrament. It is a sacramental. The Church has always set aside blessed objects to serve as sacramentals – physical, tangible, visible, blessed by the Church as a support for our faith. God's blessing and God's presence are mediated to us through things. As C.S. Lewis says:

> There is no good trying to be more spiritual than God. God never meant man to be a purely spiritual creature. That is why He uses material things like bread and wine to put new life into us. We may think this rather crude and unspiritual. God does not: He invented eating. He likes matter. He invented it.[1]

Lay people can use blessed oil in praying for healing. In the Roman Rite we had this ancient blessing for oil to be used by the laity:

> Our help is in the name of the Lord.
> *Response*: Who made heaven and earth.
> God's creature, oil,
> I cast out the demon from you
> By God the Father almighty +
> Who made heaven and earth and sea
> And all that they contain.
> Let the adversary's power, the devil's legions,
> And all Satan's attacks and machinations
> Be dispelled and driven afar from this creature oil.
> Let it bring health in body
> And mind to all who use it,
> In the name of the God +, the Father almighty,
> And of our Lord Jesus Christ +, his Son, and of the
> Holy Spirit +, the Advocate,
> As well as in the love of the same
> Jesus Christ our Lord
> Who is coming to judge both the living
> And the dead
> And the world by fire. Amen.

Lord, hear my prayer.

Response: And let my cry be heard by you.

The Lord be with you.

Response: And also with you.

Let us pray:

Lord God almighty,

Before whom the hosts of angels stand in awe

And whose heavenly service we acknowledge,

May it please you to regard favourably

And to bless and hallow this creature, oil,

Which by your power has been pressed

From the juice of olives.

You have ordained it for the anointing of the sick, so that,

When they are made well, they may give thanks to you,

The living and true God.

Grant, we pray, that those who use this oil,

Which we are blessing + in your name,

May be delivered from all suffering, all infirmity,

And all the wiles of the enemy.

Let it be a means of averting any kind of adversity

From man, made in your image and redeemed by the
   precious

Blood of your Son,

So that he may never again suffer

The sting of the ancient serpent,

Through Christ our Lord. Amen.

(The oil is sprinkled with holy water)

The priest may use this ancient blessing of the Roman Ritual, or he may use one of his own choice.

The people show by their eagerness to receive the blessing that they understand the significance of this sacramental. Having prayed for healing and opened their whole lives to the Holy Spirit, they now present themselves for an individual blessing. As people come forward to receive the blessing, the congregation sings and, what is most striking, they are happy to keep singing until the last person has been blessed. Nobody seems to be in a hurry to get away. Another striking feature of the blessing with oil is that people will go to the lay ministers without any hesitation. They recognize the ministry of their brothers and sisters. This is a clear proof that the healing gifts are in the community, that the people recognize this fact, and that the Church should be using these gifts as a normal part of its ministry. The blessing with oil is a very intimate, private moment when the person may ask for a specific grace of healing. Usually people ask for inner healing, especially within the marriage and the family. When a whole family comes forward marvellous healing of relationships takes place. Often husband and wife come forward together. Their marriage will be renewed as they ask together for healing.

On one occasion while I was leading a healing service in a parish, the parish priest, a senior man in the diocese, was judiciously trying to make up his mind about the whole thing. He was approached by a woman who asked him to bless her and pray for God to forgive her for her hatred of the Catholic Church. God had healed her during the service. All the priest's doubts were resolved!

The response to the healing service is, in itself, its own justification. The healing service is not only a great ministry to offer people but it is also a most powerful means of evangelizing. People who have given up on God and the Church for deep personal reasons will return to a Church that is offering healing in the name of the Lord. Our dream should be that in every parish, in every Christian community, whatever the denominations, people will be able to experience a ministry in the name of Jesus for the healing of the whole person.

Notes

[1] C.S. Lewis, *Mere Christianity*, New York: Macmillan, 1964.

About the author ...

Jim McManus is a Redemptorist priest based in St Mary's Renewal Centre in Perth, Scotland. His published books include:

The Healing Power of the Sacraments,

Hallowed Be Thy Name

All Generations Will Call Me Blessed: Mary at the Millennium

Deliverance Ministry in the Catholic Tradition

He served as Provincial Superior of his Congregation in Britain for nine years. He has preached retreats and conducted workshops on Healing and The Spirituality of True Self-Esteem in many parts of the world.